Chasing Dragons

The Expanded Version

Chasing Dragons

The Expanded Version

By Mark Nickless and Laurie Bonner-Nickless

Including excerpts from
To The Gates of Fengtu

Translated by Laurie Bonner-Nickless

"*To the Gates of Fengtu* is the definitive proof that China discovered America"
Gavin Menzies
author of *1421 – The Year China Discovered America*

Copyright © 2019 by Mark Nickless & Laurie Bonner-Nickless
All rights reserved.

This book or any portion thereof
may not be reproduced or used in any manner whatsoever
without the express written permission of the publisher
except for the use of brief quotations in a book review.

Printed in the United States of America

Dr. Arlan Andrews, Sr.
Acquisitions Editor
Talisman House Press
An imprint of Hydra Publications, LLC

Cover by Laurie Bonner-Nickless

Talisman House Press
Goshen, KY 40026

www.talismanhousepress.com

DEDICATION

To the men of the fleet,
And to our ancestors,
You laid the path that led to where we now stand.

To Grandpa C. S. Nickless & Grandma Faye Bonner,
Your guidance and examples put us on that path.

To Ekaterina and Samantha,
may you find what we did in this legacy,
Greater strength of purpose for the road that lies ahead.

CONTENTS

	Foreword – Lee Pennington	1
	Prologue	3
	Introduction	4
I	Marquette's Monsters	6
II	Tracking the "Devourer of Men" To Its Lair	14
III	"Der Piasa Felsen"	22
IV	July 5th, 2005, Nanjing	26
V	Semple the Destroyer	49
VI	Manifested As An Absence	55
VII	The Inscription On Fort Hill	59
VIII	Whence Wings?	66
IX	Remnants of Memory	73
X	Chinese Corroboration: Enter Luo Mao Deng	78
XI	Chinese Corroboration: The Taoist Master's Modest Proposal	83
XII	Chinese Corroboration: The Loach King	97
XIII	Chinese Corroboration: Luo's Account of the Piasa	105
XIV	A Mystery On The Periphery: The Final Proof	115
XV	A Summary Of The Work – Answers	122
XVI	Piasa Timeline and References	128
	About the Authors	137
	A Personal Connection	138
	Additional Supportive Proofs	139
	Related Reading / Related Websites	141
	Is More Evidence Out There?	142
	Bibliography	143

OUR THANKS…

To Gavin Menzies for helping to set us on this road.

To James Kennedy, our friend, you knew when a deer is not a deer.

To the long-suffering staff of Jefferson College and the
DeSoto Library for kindnesses above & beyond the call of duty…

And, to Larry Wegmann & the late Frank Magre
who found the impossible written in stone.

Editor's Note

Chasing Dragons: The Expanded Version is the first book published through Talisman House Press. As Editor, it was my pleasure to work with Mark and Laurie Nickless to present to the world and to other researchers the intriguing discoveries and fascinating insights that they have brought to light.

Many ancient mysteries of the Piasa, of Cahokia, and of Ming Dynasty exploration have now been solved, as you will read in the following pages.

Other mysteries of other times and places await, and Talisman House Press will bring them to you.

>Dr. Arlan Andrews, Sr.
>Acquisitions Editor
>Talisman House Press
>An imprint of Hydra Publications, Inc.
>Goshen, Kentucky

Foreword

I first heard of Mark and Laurie Nickless from my friend, Jim Scherz, a professor emeritus at the University of Wisconsin, and an amazing scholar and researcher.

Jim, who had visited the Nickless at their home in Illinois, was fascinated with the work they were doing concerning the possibility of the Chinese sailing to pre-Columbia America and exploring deep into the interior of the continent—with the intent to establish Buddhism among the natives.

Jim on a visit with me told about their amazing work. He said that Laurie was actually attempting to translate an overlooked Chinese diary that was written in ancient literary Mandarin, a writing even the Chinese scholars had difficulty deciphering. It seems no one around really could accurately read or translate the material.

Laurie took it on herself to learn that ancient language and to translate the last 15 chapters of that diary (*To the Gates of Fengtu* published 2017). That manuscript not only tells in detail of the Chinese being on this continent but also more than hints at the great tragedy which took place when their elaborate plan to force Buddhism on the local population went awry with disastrous consequences. The emperor who had sent them on their voyage had lost favor and was ousted, and the new emperor had the great fleet of ships burned on their return to the China mainland. All records concerning the exploration, at least most of them, were destroyed—except, that is, one lone sailor's diary which somehow had managed to survive.

Mark and Laurie began all their work on the Chinese question while attempting to research and to discover the true story behind the Piasa, a figure originally located along the cliffs beside the Mississippi River. The Piasa was first described by Father Jacques Pere Marquette in 1673 as he explored the river area south from Canada. Marquette characterized the figure as "two painted monsters which at first made us afraid." He even made a detailed sketch of the rock painting, but Marquette's illustration was lost when his canoe capsized later during the trip.

Much later than Marquette, as the figure on the stone wall weathered and deteriorated, others came up with different stories, some quite fanciful, as to what the monster was and what it represented. According to some early reports it was a figure that even the Indians feared and hated. They were often seen shooting at the figure after the arrival of the Europeans had brought them firearms.

Even the site of the original Piasa was changed and a new painting created (perhaps part of a cover up to protect historic land claims). Through the passage of time, all semblance of reality of the figure was mostly lost and in its place was a newly created figure that had little or no connection to the original or even to its purpose. It was through some excellent historic forensic work that Mark and Laurie Nickless were able to recover a much more accurate picture and story of the Piasa.

Three years after they published *Chasing Dragons—the True History of the Piasa (2012),* we of the Ancient Kentucky Historical Association (AKHA) invited Mark and Laurie to come present their findings to our group. They had already been invited to China and had presented their work there. I had earlier purchased and read their new book and was much impressed with their discoveries.

At that AKHA meeting, I was even more impressed because what they presented showed that just since their book was published three years earlier much new supporting evidence for their hypothesis has come to light.

In fact, during the six years since release of *Chasing Dragons*, so much new information about the Piasa has presented itself that a new, updated version of the book was needed.

With so much new evidence now available that was not accessible five years ago, *Chasing Dragons--The Expanded Version* by Hydra Publications admirably fulfills that purpose.

Here on these pages you will find that history as you and I were taught simply does not hold up when confronted with a plethora of new evidence suggesting otherwise. Laurie and Mark Nickless and Hydra Publications are to be greatly commended for bringing that crucial evidence to us.

--Lee Pennington,
President, Ancient Kentucky Historical Association

Mark Nickless & Laurie Bonner-Nickless

PROLOGUE

Summary of the Work

In this book we have made known our discoveries of the answers to several historical mysteries, documenting our conclusions step-by-step. The following is a summary of the mysteries, all of which are inter-related, as we will show.

Mystery #1: What is the origin and meaning of the enigmatic *Piasa* monsters painting discovered by the explorer Marquette on a river bluff at Elsah, Illinois? And why did the *Piasa* vanish for decades, then reappear in another version in nearby Alton?

Mystery #2: Why did the population of the Mississippi Valley suffer a decimation in the mid-1400s?

Mystery #3: Is there any evidence, as claimed by Menzies and others, that the fleet of Chinese Admiral *Zheng He* visited North America in the 1400s?

Mystery #4: Why was the immense Chinese fleet burned and Chinese world exploration ended after the return of the seventh *Zheng He* global expedition?

The answers to these questions form the basis of this book.

Chasing Dragons

INTRODUCTION

In the spring of 1668, a French Jesuit missionary working with native tribes around the Great Lakes heard a rumor. To the west, it was said, was a great river, a river that split the world. Writing to his superiors, Father Jacques Marquette obtained permission to determine the truth of these rumors, and in the spring of 1673 he launched a small expedition in the company of explorer Louis Joliet. Taking with them five French-Native American "voyageurs", Marquette and Joliet set out across the treacherous waters of Lake Michigan in two birch bark canoes.

On June 17, two months after setting out, the canoes emerged from the Wisconsin River and joined the broad waters of the Mississippi. Far down river, in an area that would now be western Illinois, they made a surprising discovery unequaled by any explorer of the American continent that came after them.

Father Marquette wrote,

> "While Skirting some rocks, which by Their height and length inspired awe, we saw upon one of them two painted monsters which at first made Us afraid, and upon Which the boldest savages dare not Long rest their eyes…. Moreover, these 2 monsters are so well painted that we cannot believe that any savage is their author…"

Many poor attempts have been made to identify the creatures that this Jesuit scholar saw on that limestone bluff, but all of them have paid little attention to his original description. Perhaps that's because the image suggested by Marquette is as unsettling to historians today as it was to the region's natives back then. The monsters Marquette described were clearly dragons, and he was quite right to doubt that they had been painted by the locals. Our research proves that the painting was Chinese.

Chasing Dragons

CHAPTER I

MARQUETTE'S MONSTERS

A cross-categorical classroom is a frenetic place. It is like a robin's nest full of needy chicks, each demanding to be fed immediately by their harried parents. But, for one brief, rare moment, all my students had been attended to, and they were working on assignments. Melisa, my aide, had brought in a copy of The Jefferson County Missouri *LEADER* to read, and in it was its occasional supplement, *SENIOR TIMES*. I was over 50, so I gave it a quick glance. I noticed an article about a local mystery – the Piasa – which had once been a magnificent painting of two monstrous creatures, high on a bluff overlooking the Mississippi River, above St. Louis. It was discovered in 1673, by the Jesuit explorer, Jacques Marquette.

The Piasa's origin was a mystery to Marquette, and surprisingly, to the Indians accompanying him. I thought the story was interesting, so I made a mental note of it before plunging back into reality. But it refused to stay in the back of my mind. Repeatedly, the Piasa story kept resurfacing. "This is tied into something else I know," I kept thinking. Finally, it added up. A few days before, late in the evening, I had crashed on the couch; wanting nothing more than to mindlessly channel-surf. I stumbled upon an elderly gentleman speaking on C-SPAN's Book Television. His name was Gavin Menzies, and he was talking about his new book, *1421-The Year China Discovered America*. Menzies claimed that decades before Columbus, the Ming Chinese had built a great fleet of massive ships that mapped the world, including North America.

Ming Chinese explorers in America? Where was the proof? Wait, weren't dragons a Chinese symbol, and didn't they portray them in pairs? I searched for "Piasa" on the internet. I quickly found

Marquette's original description:
Father Marquette wrote,

> While skirting some rocks, which by their height and length inspired awe, we saw upon one of them two painted monsters which at first made us afraid, and upon which the boldest savages dare not long rest their eyes. They are large as a calf; they have horns on their heads like those of a deer, a horrible look, red eyes, a beard like a tiger's, a face somewhat like a man's, a body covered with scales, and so long a tail that it winds all around the body, passing above the head and going back between the legs, ending in a fish's tail. Green, red, and black are the three colors composing the picture. Moreover, these 2 monsters are so well painted that we cannot believe that any savage is their author; for good painters in France would find it difficult to reach that place conveniently to paint them. Here is approximately the shape of these monsters, as we have faithfully copied it."

Ironically, Marquette's sketch of the monsters was reportedly lost some weeks later on his return to French-controlled Canada, when his canoe was swamped in the LaChine, or Chinese Rapids of the St Lawrence River. The origin of this unusual name has been lost over time, but it hints that 17th century French explorers believed the St. Lawrence River had a connection to China.

Obviously, Marquette was very impressed. I had to take him at his word — the Piasa was not the work of American Indians. If it was not painted by my great-great grandfather's people, then who did? Perhaps, was the Piasa a pair of Chinese dragons? I realized then how little I knew about Chinese dragons. It was then that I began to seriously research this mystery.

I soon found that the Chinese called their dragons *"lóng"*, and that their characteristics were by no means the same as those of dragons from European mythologies. A *"lóng"* was wingless and benign. It was not the enemy of man, but the living symbol of Imperial China. It had a snake's body with scales, a tail like a fish, antlers like a deer, and – wait a minute — this internet article concerning the Chinese *lōng* could have been written by Marquette describing the Piasa.

I showed my notes to Laurie. She responded by rummaging through her jewelry box, quickly pulling out a Chinese bracelet. She eyed it carefully for a moment and then handed it to me; I stared down at the suddenly very familiar image of a dragon decorating it, and then she said, "Go for it."

Over the next few days, I continued to find additional similarities between a *lōng* and the Piasa. I soon had eleven:

1. The Piasa was actually a pair of creatures, typical in a Chinese *lōng* motif.

2. Both creatures had horns like deer.

3. Both had red fiery demon eyes.

4. Both had a beard or whiskers like a tiger's.

5. Both were covered with scales.

6. Both were painted in green, red, and black. These are Imperial colors and can be seen today on Chinese New Year's dragons.

7. Both possessed long, sinuous tails long enough to wrap around their bodies.

8. Both of their tails terminated in a fish's tail.

9. Both had human-like faces. In the emblem of China's first emperor, *Qin Shi Huang Di*, the

face was that of a magical beast, the *quillin*, which is traditionally depicted with human-like facial features.

10. An absence of wings. This would be unusual in a Western dragon. Traditionally, many Chinese dragons flew without wings.

11. Both exhibited highly sophisticated execution, as good as any in France, what you would expect from the technically advanced Chinese. No other pictographs are known that approached this level of skill.

This many parallels could hardly be mere coincidence. Here was the evidence for a Chinese origin for the Piasa. And I was not the first to conclude this; in the 1880's, Banker George H. Dougherty[1] discovered jade items in an Indian burial mound along Piasa Creek, near its mouth on the Mississippi River in Illinois. He believed that they were of Chinese origin, and tied them into Marquette's description of the Piasa.

In 1924, another banker, E. W. Payne[2], independently reached the same conclusion: "A superficial examination of the painting" – and there is one that survives — "shows that it is undoubtedly a Chinese dragon." Payne theorized that the Chinese had reached the Midwest from the Pacific using Indian trails. He also believed it was a one-way trip by the forlorn crew of a wrecked ship.

---

[1] https://jersey.illinoisgenweb.org/newspaper/clippings2.htm
[2] https://greenfreelibrary.newspaperarchive.com/wellsboro-gazette/1924-12-04/page-3/

Chasing Dragons

We have personally seen the two jade artifacts. One is a small circular disc with a hole at the center. The larger piece is oblong, about four inches in length. They are presently kept in a small museum in Otterville, Illinois. An old newspaper clipping about them has been partially preserved, but incredibly in mid-sentence, the article is continued on to another page, which is missing!

The jade objects in Illinois (foreground) are resting on graph paper marked in sq. cm.

The article does speculate that the jade could have come from Mayan lands in Central America. This possible Mayan connection will become important later in this book, as we shall see.

Both Dougherty and Payne were men of solid judgment and intellectual curiosity. To their advantage, they both worked banker's hours, thus having the time and money to do thorough research. Sadly, this rational view of the Piasa's origin has been preempted to this day, in the public's eye, by a pseudo-legend of great staying power.

Beginning in 1836, Professor John Russell[3] published a series

---

[3] *THE PIASA* or *THE DEVIL AMONG THE INDIANS*, Morris, ILL., E.B. Fletcher, Book and Job Printer, 1887

of articles that purported to be a recounting of an Indian legend that explained the Piasa. They were written in the romantic Victorian style of his day, heavily laced with moral instruction, and found a ready audience in religious publications. Russell transformed Marquette's two wingless monsters into a single giant bird, and claimed that Piasa meant "beast that devours men" in the Illinois Indian language. (Never mind that the Indians said the Piasa painting was already there when they first arrived in that region!) This Piasa bird preyed upon the Indians and left their skeletons piled in its lair – a ghastly cave high on an imposing cliff. The Piasa was eventually killed through trickery. Chief Ouatoga offered himself up as a sacrifice to the Piasa, but when the creature swooped down to pounce upon him; his concealed braves suddenly unleashed a barrage of poisoned arrows, killing it.

Dry facts could never compete with that.

Within a few days of beginning my research into the Piasa, there occurred one of the most extreme examples of synchronicity I have ever experienced. We received an unsolicited e-mail from Carl M., a Mensa acquaintance of ours. He is an expert linguist, speaking Mandarin Chinese and several Native American languages, among others. He had edited and published an exhaustive Kaskaskia Illinois-to-French Dictionary. Laurie had earned Carl's gratitude by digitally restoring an old painting, which became his cover art. Carl regularly sent stimulating linguistic tidbits to his circle of somewhat eccentric friends. Incredibly, the subject of this e-mail was the meaning of the word "Piasa," which has traditionally been held to mean "destroyer" or "devourer of men." However, his research had led him to conclude that, in the original Indian language, "Piasa" actually referred to a "water elf" or "dwarf"… little people! For Carl, this only deepened the mystery of the Piasa, for it did not fit the conventionally accepted story. But to me, it was a revelation.

"Piasa" could refer, not to painted beasts, but to their creators—small men. (It must be kept in mind that the men of some local tribes, such as the Osage, averaged well over six feet in height—giants in their day.) Chinese explorers, men of relatively slight stature, had painted their national emblem on a prominent bluff in a new land.

It all made sense.

It is difficult to sit on a powerful idea like this. Fortunately, I had a ready venue in which to publish my research.

In 1971, I graduated with Bob Whitehead, from Crystal City High School. Bob had become editor of *OUTDOOR GUIDE MAGAZINE*, a regional hunting and fishing publication, based in St. Louis. My twin outdoor passions are wet-wade fishing for trout in small streams and paddling my 9-foot Otter™ kayak in pursuit of the toothy chain pickerel, a small but ferocious cousin of the Northern pike. Few highs can match hooking into a state-record-class pickerel and being towed in circles on a crystal-clear Ozark mountain lake in winter. It was natural then that I would contribute the occasional fishing article to the *"OGM,"* as we called it. *OGM* did publish an occasional local history piece, and Bob owed me a few favors, so I sent him a short article sharing my insight into the Piasa's origin. Bob published my piece in his October/November 2004 issue.

Surprisingly, he wrote a brief commentary predicting that my research would lead somewhere important. Disappointingly, the positive feedback I had innocently expected did not immediately materialize. I concluded that this was the end of my research into the Piasa—and went back to writing fishing articles.

Then a few days later, in the evening, our phone rang.

The voice on the other end was unfamiliar and accented. The conversation that followed was totally unexpected. The caller identified himself as Bill Wu, a geneticist at Washington University, in St. Louis, Missouri. He wanted to share some important news with us. A big event was being planned for Nanjing, China — a celebration of the 600th anniversary of the first voyage of the great Ming fleet of 1405, commanded by the legendary Admiral Zheng He. The proceedings would include a history conference, and there was a call for papers about Chinese exploration. Bill invited me to expand my original short article into a full research paper, which he offered to translate and submit to the proper authorities.

This was a bolt out of the blue.

What had just happened?

Later, we learned how Jim Kennedy, a close friend of Bill, had run across my article while reading the *OUTDOOR GUIDE MAGAZINE*. Jim quickly shared it with Bill, who is from mainland China. Bill knew of the celebration in Nanjing, and was well-connected.

For him, this was his opportunity to earn some "face" back home. For my family and me, the direction of our lives had just changed forever.

The next few months were filled with activity. In addition to teaching school, there was research and writing to do, and a frenetic road trip to Chicago to obtain a visa from the Chinese consulate.

One unresolved mystery about the Piasa was its exact location. Unfortunately, it had been assaulted by centuries of gunfire; first by newly-armed Indians whose collective memory dimly remembered that it was foreign, and then by whites who despised it because they thought it was Indian. Sometime in the mid-nineteenth century, the limestone bluff on which it was painted was quarried for building material. Once obliterated, its precise location was forgotten. "Somewhere near the junction of the Illinois and Mississippi Rivers" was all that was remembered.

The Piasa's location and its physical appearance was further obscured in 1925 when a large and garish new Piasa, copied from the cover artwork of an 1897 Hapgood Plow Company catalog, was painted prominently above the Great River Road in Alton, Illinois, some 15 miles south of the rivers' junction. It had absurdly large antlers, a whip tail and huge wings.

Sadly, this is the image of the Piasa as a giant man-eating bird—Marquette's eyewitness description notwithstanding—has remained in the public's eye to this day and has been relocated so as to be better seen by tourists.

To further our research, we had to track down the Piasa's original location. In time, we found our quarry—at a quarry.

CHAPTER II

TRACKING THE "DEVOURER OF MEN" TO ITS LAIR

In March, 2005, Bill Wu contacted us with a modest proposal. He and Jim Kennedy wanted to find the original Piasa site.

On Saturday, March 19th, our dragon hunting expedition—Jim, Bill and I—left St. Louis and crossed over the Mississippi River on the marvelously engineered Clark Bridge into Alton, Illinois. Then we turned north onto the Great River Road. It is certainly appropriately named. It was built in stages, first as a bed for railroad tracks; then a roadway for vehicles was added in the 1930s. All were laid down on top of several feet of gravel fill poured directly on top of the riverbed of the Mississippi. We drove past riverboat casinos and grain silos, then past the abominable Piasa Bird painting. After enduring the vision of that embarrassment, we began our search along the great bluffs for which the River Road is justly famous.

Fittingly, our quarry was the quarry which our research indicated was the site of the original Piasa before its deliberate destruction. As Jim drove, William and I craned our necks to search to the right and upward. Pale buff-colored bluffs towered over us for mile after mile. Finally, we spotted a break in the continuous line of bluffs, which might have been a quarry. However, we were not where accepted history placed the Piasa. We were well north of Alton, near a small collection of old stone houses. We pulled onto the road's shoulder and stiffly exited Jim's vehicle into a cold March wind that flowed down the river from the north and made a lie of the 40-degree temperature on the thermometer. We climbed up a slight rise into a wilderness of scrubby brush and limestone rubble that had been piled to the east of the Great River Road during it construction.

About fifty yards in front of us, the bluff towered upward, nearly a hundred feet. We had been correct in our first impression.

This was obviously the site of an old quarry. Grooves left behind by vertical drilling were clearly visible. We decided this site showed a lot of promise, but we did not know if there were any other quarries in the area.

After a brief conference, we loaded up again and continued northward. The steep bluffs soon began to shrink and eventually dwindled away completely into gentle rolling hills near Pere Marquette State Park. We were clearly beyond our search area, and somewhat surprisingly, we had not seen any sign of another quarry. We turned around and drove back south toward Alton.

Once we reached Alton, we continued southward, doing so for two reasons. First, we wanted to see if there were any bluffs south of Alton. Second, we wanted to locate the point where the Mississippi and the Missouri join to become the mighty lower Mississippi. We knew that some had claimed the Piasa was a navigation marker constructed by local natives to warn of the dangerous currents caused by the wild Missouri's entrance into the more placid Mississippi. This idea had struck me as a bit silly. I enjoy kayaking, and I can "read water." I knew that flowing water changes constantly and must be judged with one's own eyes. Why any Indian tribe would invest several man-years of labor into building the Piasa for this purpose was beyond me. A pile of stones or a bent tree along the bank would have been a sufficient warning, and could have been easily relocated as conditions changed. As it turned out, the navigation marker theory was based on an ignorance of geography. There were no bluffs at the junction. The land was flat, lightly industrialized bottom land nestled behind a long protective levee.

Now that we had our answers, we turned northward once more. Shortly after passing through Alton, we were reminded why experienced researchers take field notes. Embarrassingly, after so many hours on the road, all the bluffs looked alike. We had forgotten the location of our quarry. It was time to turn to our ace-in-the-hole: a copy of a little known 1847 Henry Lewis lithograph of the Piasa.

Chasing Dragons

James handed me a murky copy that he had found on *Mysterious World* – an on-line magazine.[4] We decided to use it as a guide. Lewis had given us several clues. In the right foreground was the Piasa, painted within a large, flattened arch. In the background to the left of the picture, a low ridge appeared, punctuated by two subtle peaks. To the left, there was a sandbar "island," covered with trees. We decided to ignore the island. Such islands in the Mississippi are ephemeral, undergoing radical changes with every passing flood. We instead would concentrate our attention on the distinctive ridge line. We knew it was a risk. Many had long dismissed this particular work of Lewis as "fanciful." His accuracy would be tested now. We suffered several false alarms as we sighted hills in the distance as we rounded bends in the road.

Finally, a low ridge swung into view before us that looked

---

[4] www.mysteriousworld.com/Journal/1999/Summer/Piasa02/

right…very right. The landscape we were seeing through the windshield and the picture in my hands had become one.

We immediately pulled off and stopped at a pocket parking lot situated at the entrance to the historic village of Elsah, 10.9 miles north of the infamous Piasa painting in Alton. We were no more than one hundred yards south of where we had stopped before. Before us was a limestone quarry, the only quarry we had found.

Lewis' landscape was absolutely accurate. Could his depiction of the remains of the Piasa be any less so? Jim, ever a man of action, circled south to the back side of the quarry where the bluff mellowed into a climbable hill which he proceeded to ascend.

Bill and I jaunted east into Elsah. We quickly discovered that all of the village's older homes and public buildings were constructed of native limestone from the quarry. One local man that I met as he was retrieving a newspaper, marveled, "They were giving it away for free!" referring to land. Soon, we found ourselves

Chasing Dragons

in front of the tiny Elsah Museum, a charmingly run-down old schoolhouse. We were disappointed to discover that it was closed and would not re-open until April. Shortly, Jim returned from his climb to report that he had found an old triangular pit atop the bluff. While we found nothing spectacular, we had identified the original Piasa site. On the way home, we had some very interesting conversations while we ate Mexican food in Alton. After the three of us parted ways and I returned home, I went on the internet to do some research into Elsah's history. I discovered that while Elsah was founded in 1847 [5], its permanent structures were in fact constructed from locally limestone, quarried beginning in 1852 or 1853. It was about this time that the Piasa site was turned into a limestone quarry, and destroyed.

On the first Sunday afternoon in April, I drove my entire

---

[5] https://www.newspapers.com/clip/11727649/elsah_founding_alton_23_dec_1853/

family, Laurie, and our young daughters, Ekaterina and Samantha, to Elsah. Spring had definitely arrived. The day was warm, and the trees were erupting in brilliantly green new leaves. Elsah's riverside location makes it a perfect picture postcard place.

Postcard of the Piasa Bluffs from 1914

Even so early in the season, sleek sailboats were already gliding up and down the great river. As she watched the white-sailed vessels skim by, Laurie wondered aloud what her Osage ancestors, who to this day claim descent from Illinois' mound builders, must have thought when they caught their first glimpse of one of the smaller Chinese vessels rounding a bend on the Mississippi. How utterly alien those strangers must have seemed! Soon, we turned right, off the Great River Road, into Elsah. I carefully guided our Jetta through the narrow streets, past homey bed-and-breakfasts sprinkled throughout Elsah, and parked in a tiny slot in front of the venerable one-room museum.

Two obviously bored teenage girls were staffing the museum that day. They were happy to have visitors; our arrival broke their monotony. They knew little of Elsah's history, but in any event, that proved to be no obstacle. Rummaging through the clutter of memorabilia of better times, I stumbled upon a Piasa Bluffs Hotel menu, hidden directly beneath an antique kerosene lamp. Judging by the water rings around the lamp's base, and the way layers of glass cleaner had "glued" that lamp to the top of the display case; the lamp had not been shifted even an inch in many years. Moving it was well worth the open dismay of the girls manning the museum. The menu was dated 1897, decades before the painting of the abominable Piasa, at Alton.

Continuing our search, Laurie delved into a shelf laden with aging copies of ladies' church association cookbooks and self-published local guidebooks. Such small domestic histories can often provide surprising insights into earlier times. Laurie examined a copy of Elsah: a Historic Guidebook that appeared to have been waiting for us for decades among the dusty volumes. Its pages contained a detailed copy of an old area map, with Piasa Bluffs clearly marked above the site of the quarry.

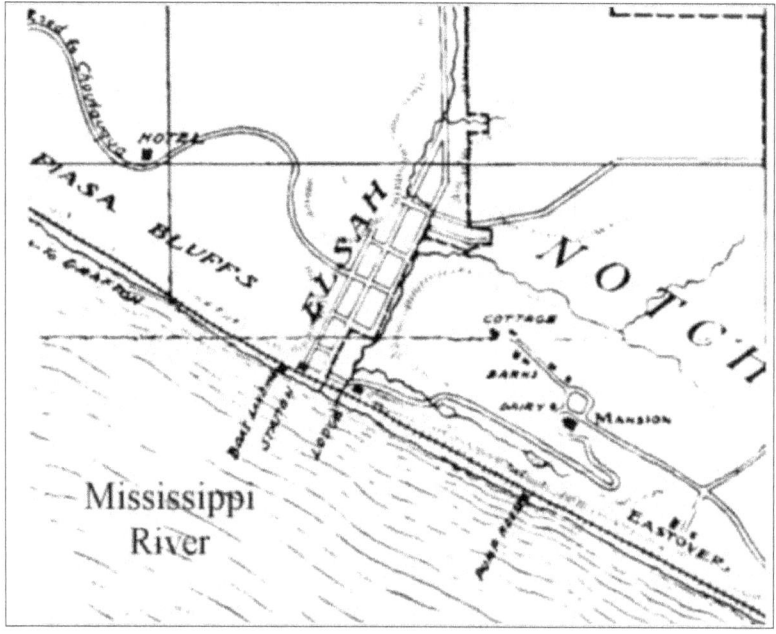

Here was our evidence, in black and white, that the location of Marquette's Piasa was known in the nineteenth century. And yet, somehow it had been quickly forgotten, and then reborn on another bluff, in an ugly, mutated form. Russell's stories of the Piasa "bird" and its later association with commercial ventures in Alton had obscured the truth until the myth had completely swallowed up the facts. But, truth is hard to hide forever. It was time to slay Russell's great beast and restore to Marquette's lost dragons the honor they deserved.

CHAPTER III

"DER PIASA FELSEN"

Things continued to happen very quickly in the spring of 2005, as we prepared our paper for its presentation in Nanjing in July. Between our first and second visits to Elsah, Laurie began searching for a crisp copy of Henry Lewis' painting of the Piasa. After consulting with the Library of Congress, she found one, in of all places, in the library at Washington University, St. Louis. We could scarcely believe our luck; it was only an hour's drive away. After getting only slightly lost, we arrived at the Washington University campus on yet another sunny Saturday morning.

The campus was charming. It had an Old World look that made us feel as if we had traveled across the Atlantic to Oxford or Cambridge, rather than driven an hour from our rural home. We spoke to a young woman briefly, and in a few moments she returned with a thick volume, cradled in her gloved hands. She laid it out reverently on a heavy wooden table in a semi-private viewing room. It was an 1854 first edition, in the original German. *Das Illustrierte Mississippithal*, or *The Illustrated Mississippi Valley*, portrays, in art and essay, the Mississippi Valley of the 1840s. Henry Lewis was a notable American artist; some of his work can be seen in the St. Louis Art Museum even today. He richly illustrated his book with lithographs of his beautiful paintings of breathtaking scenery and Westward Expansion.

Included among those illustrations was "Der Piasa Felsen," or "The Piasa Rock." That painting was done between 1846 and 1848 when Lewis sketched scenes along the upper Mississippi.[6] It is the only known depiction of the Piasa in its original, albeit tattered, glory. Sadly, the Piasa was utterly destroyed with systematic thoroughness shortly thereafter. (There was a good reason for its destruction, in the eyes of some, and we will address this later.) With great care we leafed through this copy of *Das Illustrierte Mississippithal* until we found Lewis' Piasa painting. We examined "Der Piasa Felsen" with a combination of curiosity and reverence. Laurie precisely framed the page and took several photos for later examination.

We were immediately struck by the dissonance of the elements in the image. Lewis, with the near-photographic presentation he has been noted for elsewhere, presents an upstream view with the Mississippi River on the left, balanced by a massive bluff on the right. Centered in the bluff is a massive arch, carved into a man-made stone recess. However, within that arch are disjointed body parts; some well-executed, and some very crude. On the left is a devilish human face. In the center is a bizarre winged creature with a cartoonish smile.

Our first impression was that many of those fragments appear to have been crudely added to it at different times, possibly by vandals, or even by well-meaning "restorers." It was a bit of a disappointment. Later, as we re-examined our photographs of "Der Piasa Felsen" at home, we realized that much more of Marquette's original vision remained than we had at first realized. The Piasa was painted on a painstakingly prepared surface. Lewis's painting shows a vertical limestone bluff that had been hewn back several feet and then smoothed to produce a flat, vertical arch at least 50' in height and 75' to 100' in width. Since Native Americans have not been known to use arches in the construction of their monuments and

---

[6] Lewis, Henry. "Der Pias Felen," *DAS ILLUSTRIERTE MISSISSIPPITHAL*, (Dusseldorf:Arnz & Company,1854.)
 Translated from the German by A.Hermina Poatgieter. Minnesota Historical Society,1967

great structures elsewhere, why would they carve such an immense one like this in the face of the bluff? A thick limestone outcropping immediately to the left of that arch gives a clear impression of how much material had to be quarried and removed as part of the construction process.

There were sets of unusual, parallel, diagonal grooves running from the top right to the bottom left on that outcropping. Only tough metal tools, made expressly for stone carving, could have cut those deep grooves. This seemed to be clear evidence supporting our conclusion that the local Native Americans could not have prepared that bluff face for painting. They did not possess the technology to craft such tools. Their metallurgy at that time was confined to beating or smelting bits of copper into small ornamental pieces. Nor were they known as workers of massive stone; their glory was in raising massive mounds using nothing more than humble baskets of earth.

Another fascinating detail we saw was the two Indians in the foreground. We had originally thought that they are pointing at the Piasa. But, no. Clearly, this pair of men was shooting at it. This explained why so much of the upper part of the Piasa image had been obliterated. These natives feared and hated it. When they obtained firearms, they had the opportunity to act on those emotions! At this point, we realized that in "Der Piasa Felsen" was more proof of the non-Native American origin of the Piasa.

Over the next few years, this image would slowly reveal more of its secrets. But for the moment, we had made several important discoveries which we could quickly incorporate into our paper, as our deadline was looming. Unless we completed and submitted a well-written paper, our hopes to attend the festivities in Nanjing would come to naught. One other thing had to be completed quickly. Using "Der Piasa Felsen" as a template, Laurie exercised her considerable artistic skills to reconstruct what she believed then had once decorated the space inside the unusual arch depicted by Lewis. Within the arch, she placed an image based on two carefully crafted clay Chinese *lóng* that she had manipulated until their sinuous bodies — heads, legs and tails — fit into positions that matched, as best possible, the fragmentary creatures in the painting. Eventually, she was satisfied with the accuracy of her efforts.

Laurie then produced a full color sketch that nicely blended Marquette's two original monsters into Lewis' work. It was this interpretation of the Piasa that we used as part of our research paper which we presented July, 2005, in Nanjing, China. We were not yet ready to claim that this interpretation of the Piasa was completely accurate, given the damaged state it was in when portrayed by Lewis. The hazy general outline of two huge and sinuous bodies was obvious enough, but we were not quite sure yet about how to best arrange the tails and legs, and Laurie was also troubled by not finding any clear sign of a pearl, which her own research seemed to indicate "had to" have been included in the original design.

But the answer to that question was clearly not going to be found in time to be incorporated into our first reconstruction. And there was no way we could have predicted then that the answers were waiting for us, hidden in plain sight, half a world away.

CHAPTER IV

JULY 5TH, 2005, NANJING

On to China…

Heart-breaking flight delays greatly prolonged our expected twenty-four hours of travel. And no sooner than we had finally succeeded in finding our hotel, dropped off our battered luggage, and grabbed a few bites of food, than we discovered to our great dismay that we had unwittingly missed participating in the conference's opening festivities and group photo. And then, before we knew what was happening, we were flung headlong into a day of rapid-fire stops on a high-speed tour around the city of Nanjing.

That ancient city and the surrounding country were gorgeous. The air of China smelled like spice. The people of Nanjing were wonderful, and incredibly patient with this pair of pitifully out-of-place Americans who did not know how to say anything in Mandarin beyond counting to ten, saying "please," "thank you," "yes," "no," "I'm sorry," and "I don't understand," and neither of whom could read a single word in any form of that language. Our tour buses entered a relatively small and unimposing family compound in the hills just outside the city. The crowd was very quiet. Our tour guide, Gabriel, spoke fluent English, and explained to us where we were and what was going on.

This was the home of the Zheng family line and had been since the days of Zheng He. It had been the home of the nephew the eunuch admiral had adopted as his heir. We and the rest of the participants in the conference had come to lay flowers on the cenotaph[7] erected as a memorial to the great mariner.

---

7   Empty tomb

This cenotaph had never held more than a pair of Zheng He's shoes and a lock of hair—any trace of which had been lost during the Cultural Revolution when the original tomb was smashed by the Red Guards. A gong was struck, and the entire crowd, still reverently quiet, bowed three times. Then, we left. As we boarded our bus to go back to the hotel, it suddenly felt like everything we had learned in the course of research was so much more personal.

The next morning, we walked the short distance from the Zhongshan Hotel to Room 302 of Building Number One. Incredibly, it proved to be a former temple to the God of War that dated back to the Ming Dynasty and that was now the hotel's conference building. According to a guidebook we bought later, it was also the former site of Academic Examination during the days of the Republic of China and President Sun Yat-Sen. For several hours we sat at the end of a long table, politely drinking loose tea, as speaker after speaker presented their papers in Chinese, of which we understood nothing. Then, mid-afternoon, a crowd began to gather on our right, near the entrance to the room. Some of them carried video cameras, some carried still cameras, and others carried neither. We had no clue who they were or what they were waiting for. We guessed them to be students from local universities, or part of the standard press contingent covering the Special Sessions groups of the academic forum. Laurie wondered why they seemed to be taking so few notes or pictures. When our turn finally arrived, Fan Weizhi, a fellow presenter, helped Laurie get the video portion of our presentation up and running, while I conferred a few more moments with a lady who had volunteered to translate. And then, with a nervous "*Ni hao*," I began to read, pausing periodically to allow that good lady to catch up with her echo of my words in Mandarin:

Former Temple to the God of War

Mark Nickless & Laurie Bonner-Nickless

MING EXPLORATION IN THE CENTRAL MISSISSIPPI VALLEY

The geographical extent of the travels of Zheng He's fleet have become a source of world-wide debate since the publication of Gavin Menzies' controversial *1421, the Year the Chinese Discovered America.*

Our own research, based on historical documents, had uncovered multiple lines of evidence that compel us to reach this conclusion: some of the great admiral's explorers reached the state of Illinois, in the central Mississippi Valley of North America. In 1673, the French Jesuit, Pierre Marquette, and the French-Canadian, Louis Joliet, descended the Mississippi River in the first European exploration of the Middle Mississippi Valley. As they approached the site of present day Alton, Illinois, they were thunderstruck by an unexpected and fearsome sight. Awe-inspired, Father Marquette wrote:

> "Comme nous Conoions des roches affreux pour Leur haulteur et pour leuer Longour; Nous vismes sur un de ces roches deux monstres en peinture qui Nous firent peur d'abord et sur Lesquels les sauuages les plus hardys n'osent pas arrester Longtemps les yeux; ils sent gros Comme vn veau. Ils ont des Comes en teste Comme des cheureils; un regard affreux, des yeux rouges, une barbe Comme d'un tygre, la face a quelque chose l'homme, le corps. Couuert d'ecailes, et La queued si Longue qu'elle fait tout bu Corps passant par dessus la teste et retournant entre les jambes elle se termine en queu5 de Poisson. Le vert, Le rouge et Le noirastre sont le trois Couleurs qui Le Composent: au reste ces 2

monstres sont si bien que nous ne pouuons pas croire qu'aucun sauuage en soit L'autheur, puisque Les bons peintres en fiancé auroient peine a si bien faire, veuque d'aillers ils sont si hauts sur rocher qu'il est difficile d'y atteindre Commodement pour les peindre. voicy a peu pres La figure de ces monstres Comme nous L'auons Contretiree".

"While skirting some rocks which by their height and length inspired awe, We saw upon one of them two painted monsters which at first made Us afraid, and upon Which the boldest savages dare not Long rest their eyes. They are as large as a calf; they had Horns on their heads like those of a deer, a horrible look, red eyes, a beard like a tiger's a face somewhat like a man's, a body Covered with scales, and so Long a tail that it winds all around the Body, passing above the head and going back between the legs, ending in a Fish's tail. Green, red and black are the three Colors composing the picture. Moreover, these 2 monsters are so well painted that we cannot believe that any savage is their author; for good painters in France would find it difficult to paint so well, and besides, they are so high up on the rock that it is difficult to reach the place Conveniently to paint them. Here is approximately The shape of these monsters, As we have faithfully Copied them."

Sadly, Marquette's original sketches were lost when his canoe sank near Montreal, Canada. His creatures would later come to be known by their Illinois Indian name, Piasa. Over the centuries, the Piasa weathered and faded. In the early nineteenth century, amateur attempts were made to repaint it. These efforts were fanciful, little better than vandalism, and in no way faithful to Marquette's original description. The final indignity came in 1847,[8] when the site was quarried—supposedly to make lime—and utterly destroyed. The Piasa was an enigma, its origin unknown. In place of facts, legends evolved. Ones that became greatly embellished as time passed.

In 1836, Professor John Russell wrote imaginative articles that transformed Marquette's pair of monsters in the Piasa painting into one "Bird that Devours Men," that nested in a cave heaped high with the bones of its human prey. In this manufactured "myth," the newly fledged Piasa destroyed Indian villages and ate their inhabitants. The creature was eventually destroyed by Ouatoga, a clever chief of the Illinois tribe, who bravely used himself as bait to lure the Piasa within the range of his braves' poisoned arrows.

Sadly, Professor Russell's wildly romanticized "legend" was typical of the widespread practice of Victorian scholars and scientists who embellished, and thus "improved" upon their findings. Russell's retelling utterly ignored Marquette's description of two scaly creatures, neither of which he described as winged. (In fact, Russell later told his son, Spencer, that he had made up the story.) Yet, in this fantastical form, the Piasa would become Alton's claim to fame, a local mystery whose origin has been obscured by romantic nineteenth century disinformation—until now.

An unlikely turn of events, and a book by Gavin

---

8 Later, further research would prove the year in which the Piasa was destroyed to actually have been 1857.

Chasing Dragons

Menzies, a retired Royal Navy submarine commander and expert navigator, inspired us to research the Piasa's origin. Menzies wrote: *1421: The Year the Chinese Discovered America.* In this groundbreaking book, Menzies did an exhaustive research of records, maps, charts, and archaeological discoveries from around the world. He made a startling claim, at least to western minds. According to official Chinese historical records, in June of 1406 (in Chinese history, the year of Yong Le), the Emperor Zhu Di appointed Zheng He as admiral of a great Chinese fleet.

By the great emperor's audacious command, Zheng He's fleet set sail to systematically explore the entire world. The fleet consisted of more than two-hundred four-hundred-eighty-foot long capital ships and scores of ninety-foot auxiliaries, crewed by 27,000 sailors and soldiers. Zheng He and his fleets voyaged seven times during twenty-eight years. Based on many investigations, Menzies concluded that Chinese fleets traveled the entire world, from the southern tip of Greenland, within the Arctic Circle, southward to the equally frigid coast of Antarctica. They mapped nearly the entire world. The Americas were mapped in a 1421-1423 expedition.

However, very unfortunately, after the seventh voyage, the Ming government suddenly issued an edict prohibiting all future voyages, and ordering the destruction of the remaining great ships. The maps, charts and records—purchased at a fearful cost in human lives—were gathered up and burned (save a precious few). If not for this unimaginable disaster, Zheng He's great and costly achievement would have enabled China to dominate the globe. So far, no one can be certain why the Ming government did this; it is a mystery. Because of this ill-advised decision, China then vanished as a player from the world stage for half a millennium.

Menzies believes that some of the records from Zheng He's voyages survived and made their way into Western hands. Columbus, Magellan, and other early European explorers made cryptic references to ancient maps and charts. Menzies claims that these could only have been Chinese. If he is correct, the entire Western world owes a great debt to the sacrifices of Zheng He's men.

Menzies believes he has identified an ancient map, dated in 1428, that shows part of North America's Eastern coast, including the Gulf of St. Lawrence, which is the water route from the Atlantic Ocean to the Great Lakes. It is possible then, that one of Zheng He's naval units could have used this route to reach the location of Marquette's twin monsters. A voyage from Lake Michigan to Alton, Illinois, would have required a short portage to the Illinois River, which then flows to the Mississippi River, near the location of the Piasa.

It is also possible that the Chinese came up the Mississippi from the Caribbean Sea, through the Gulf of Mexico. Menzies reports considerable evidence of a Chinese presence in the Caribbean. However, the question remained open, has there ever been any verifiable proof that Zheng He's men actually reached the center of North America? We believe that Marquette's vivid eyewitness description of the Piasa provides the final and affirmative answer to this question.

For, as described by Marquette, the earliest of Western witnesses, the Piasa is clearly a *lóng*, the personal emblem of Huang Di, the now near-mythical Yellow Emperor of China. The *lóng* was the symbol of all following Emperors and of Imperial China for four thousand years. The *lóng* is a distinctive composite beast, composed of the assimilated symbols of conquered peoples. At minimum there are 11 identical features *vis-à-vis* Marquette's monsters and the Chinese Imperial *lōng*, which is to the Westerner, a pair of dragons:

1. The Piasa is actually a pair of creatures, typical in a Chinese *lōng* motif.

2. Both creatures have horns like a deer. Marquette, in his description, did not compare the monsters' horns to any of the American deer species, all of which have wide, many pronged antlers, but he used the French word for the Eurasian roebuck, which has spike horns. This species of deer is found in Europe, Siberia, and China.

At this point, I deviated from our printed report, and Laurie brought up on the screen[9] the pictures that would illustrate an important point...

---

9 This following framed section of text with pictures are recreations of the slides from our PowerPoint presentations.

"Much of the confusion in properly identifying the Piasa stemmed from those translators who mistakenly translated Marquette's words to indicate the common white tail deer of North America. Marquette *specifically* spoke of the 'cheureil' or as it is spelled today 'cheuriel,' *the roe buck.*

"Cheureil" translates as "Roe Deer"

"Cerf Communs" translates as "deer"

3. Both have a "beard" or whiskers like a tiger's.

4. Both are painted in green, red, and black; these are imperial colors.

5. Both are covered with scales.

6. Both possess long, sinuous tails, long enough to wrap around their bodies.

7. Both of their tails terminate in a fish's tail.

8. Both have human-like faces. The long has the face of a magical beast, the quillin, traditionally depicted with human-like facial features, creations of the screens from our video presentation.

9. Both demonstrate an absence of wings. This would be unusual in a Western dragon.

10. Highly sophisticated execution, "as good as any in France," precisely what you would expect from the technologically advanced Chinese.

11. Both have red, fiery, demon eyes. (This characteristic is present in some *lōng* representations, not all.)

These numerous identical characteristics should serve to positively identify Marquette's two intertwined beasts as the emblem of Imperial China. Our research has uncovered additional several lines of evidence that also point to this conclusion. Recently, a more precise translation of the Illinois Indian word "Piasa" was made. "Piasa" defined as "a destroyer" or "devourer of men" in Russell's fantasy, actually referred to a "water elf" or "dwarf" … small beings closely associated with the Mississippi River. (It must be kept in mind that many men of the local Native American tribes, such as the Osage, stood well over six feet [nearly two meters] in height—giants in their day. The average Chinese male during the Ming period averaged 5'2" to 5'5" [1.6 to 1.65 meters]).

Mark Nickless & Laurie Bonner-Nickless

"Piasa" then referred not to the beasts but to their creators—long forgotten artisans who created an image identical to a *lōng*. These long forgotten craftsmen could have only been Chinese. Perhaps, the principal reason the Piasa has remained an enigma for centuries is that it was believed that no reliable image of it had survived. An obscure 19th century lithograph of the Piasa does exist, but in the past it was judged wildly imaginative and inaccurate. *We disagree.* We believe it is accurate and revealing, but *misinterpreted.* We reached this conclusion after examining a copy of the rare German *first edition,* kept at Washington University, in St. Louis, Missouri.

Henry Lewis' lithograph, "Der Piasa Felsen" from Das Illustrirte Mississippithal, published in 1857.

Das Illustrirte Mississippithal (or *The Illustrated Mississippi Valley*) was published in Düsseldorf, Germany, beginning in 1854. It was richly illustrated by its author—Henry Lewis, a noted painter of the

American frontier. Included among the book's lithographic prints is "Der Piasa Felsen," a rendering of the Piasa, done in 1845,[10] when Lewis saw it firsthand. At first glance, one is struck by the scale of the smoothed rock face that served as a "canvas" for the Piasa. It is huge, perhaps fifty feet high and seventy-five to one hundred feet in width. Curiously, only the lower portion of the bluff are shown painted. Two odd figures are clearly visible, drawn in heavy, crude lines.

The right-hand one is a bizarre beast, which has been described as a bird. Indeed, it is shown with wings, but this "bird" has a very un-avian and toothsome smile on its face, and has five clawed toes. To the left, is a horned, disembodied head, which is devilish in appearance. Superficially, these creatures do not appear to form a *lōng* motif. However, careful study reveals several salient features that lead us to believe that this picture in fact contains a classic *lōng*.

First, we must return to Father Marquette's original description of what has come to be called the Piasa. Marquette describes the "two monsters" as being placed so high upon the river bluff that no savage could reach them. Yet, Lewis' Piasa is depicted as placed close to the ground, well within the reach of any vandal armed with a piece of charcoal…

(I paused and pointed to the image of Henry Lewis' lithograph.)

Clearly, these lower pictures had been redrawn. The crude wings and smiling face totally contradict Marquette's description, both in their forms and the level of artistic expertise involved. Surely, these crude

---

10 Later, additional research revealed 1846 was a more likely date.

caricatures are embellishments—poor attempts to highlight the fading remains of a pre-existing greater work. Yet even pitiful as these images now appear, they still preserve some hints of what must have originally been emblazoned across the full bluff face. The key to understanding the picture is in the freshly exposed yellow-bluff expanse of "empty" limestone above the figures in the 1854 lithograph. According to Marquette, this lofty void was once the heart of the painting. And it was, before the arrival of gunpowder.

After Native Americans obtained European firearms, they immediately set to work on defacing the Piasa with a hail of lead. One early source, Captain Amos Stoddard, commented that it seemed as if the Piasa had been hit with ten thousand bullets. Could this act of desecration have been some sort of ritualized kill as is so often seen throughout the archaeological record and in Native American religious artifacts? No wonder what the motivation behind it, may have been, this broadside of lead gradually erased the bulk of the Piasa—exposing fresh, lighter colored limestone underneath. The apparent void, then, actually locates the bulk of the two beasts' bodies. If you look carefully at the picture, you can see something vague and sinuous in the expanse of bluff-yellow limestone, a sort of negative image formed by the greatest concentration of gunfire. Indeed, Lewis clearly depicted several native men pointing their rifles directly at the Piasa. With this in mind, even in its defaced condition, several *lōng* elements can be identified in Lewis' Piasa:

1. A man-like face with horns and flowing whiskers. It is in the lower left of the depiction, where one would expect to see a *long*'s face in a typical two *lōng* motif.

2. Parts of perhaps two sinuous bodies with scales.

3. A Chinese-style fish tail that laps over the body of the right-facing lower creature.

4. Five-toed claws. The Lewis depiction clearly shows a creature with scales. (A bird would have four toes. A Native American artist, familiar with nature, would never have made this mistake.)

5. The general outline of large bodies in the upper yellow void.

With these key elements identified, the disembodied parts then fell into their proper places and enable an artist to reconstruct the lost original form. Indeed, a complete Imperial *lóng* motif can be superimposed upon those parts, complete with the appropriate pose, with the body of one of the beasts arranged head down on the left.

I paused and pointed to the screen.

"The Creation of the Piasa"[11] *(Recreation by L. L. Nickless)*

Several pieces of evidence in Lewis' painting can be found outside of the *lōng* motif itself, in the surrounding limestone. To the left of the Piasa, Lewis depicts a stone bluff that has been clearly removed by man to create the flat surface of the Piasa's "canvas." On the left, unusual quarrying marks that run at a diagonal, from top to bottom left, are clearly visible. These quarrying marks are similar to those found on some unfinished Ming-era stonework...This quarried area has weathered back to its original dark gray patina and must be very old ... The diagonal could have been chiseled by metal tools. However, this points to a non-native origin; for *the local Native Americans possessed no such tools*

---

11   This was an image that Laurie would radically change after we realized the implications of one of the photographs she had taken in one of the temples to Quan Yin the day before this presentation. That photograph held something we would not recognize for what it really was until nearly two years later.

prior to the incursion of white settlers into the region.

As is stated in the Squier's archeological report of 1847[12]; it is probably unnecessary to say, that the mound builders did not attempt the working of large stones, for building or other purposes, they occasionally broke up or quarried through the sand strata in defending their military positions, *none* of the disrupted stones bear the marks of edged tools.*

---

[12] www.siu.edu/~anthro/muller/Squier_1847.htm

NOT OF NATIVE ORIGIN

The quarrying is just one piece of evidence that points to a non-native origin. Here are others:

1. Archaeologists have examined more than seven hundred native pictographs and petroglyphs in Missouri. The state of Missouri is adjacent to the Illinois Piasa site, just a few hundred yards across the Mississippi River. The native populations of both states were ethnically and culturally virtually identical. Yet, none of this native art used the colors green or blue.

2. Spencer Russell, "Professor" Russell's son, recorded that what was left of the Piasa was carved one-half inch into the limestone, and was painted black, red, and blue...That it was carved into the stone was important. That it was blue is more curious, but perhaps also a revelation...

   Cobalt was used by the Ming Chinese to produce a range of brilliant paint pigments, including Cobalt green...After several centuries of weathering; this green would have broken down again into its blue and yellow components. The yellow pigment would have leached away over time, but the more stable cobalt compound would have survived, producing a dull blue Piasa. This blue color was described by the younger Russell as being more intense after becoming wet in the rain, again, this strongly suggests the presence of cobalt blue and only a Chinese origin can explain the green that turned to blue.

3. Native works are typically small and crude, rarely more than a few inches across. The Piasa was described as a masterpiece that equaled anything in Europe. It was no wonder then, that early witnesses attributed the Piasa to an unknown and lost civilization.

4. Lewis portrayed a Piasa that had been worked to a smooth, flat, arched vertical surface—approximately five thousand square feet in area. Producing this flat surface, the prerequisite for carving and painting the Piasa, required the removal of tons of limestone…yet again, the Squier's Archaeological report stated categorically that the native Cahokians "did not attempt the working of large stones, for building or other purposes." For this reason alone, the Piasa could not have been of Native American origin.

5. The Cahokians did not possess the necessary metal tools. The only worked metal found locally was native copper, from Lake Michigan. This was hammered into small objects, such as jewelry. Some ceremonial ax heads have been unearthed, made from single, large copper nuggets. However, metal smelting was unknown to Mississippian cultures.

At this point, Laurie summoned up a picture that was one of the primary arguments that had been for *a native origin for the Piasa. It was laughable to equate this crude and comparatively tiny beast with the vastly larger and more sophisticated Piasa from Lewis' lithograph.*

6. There are no truly comparable Piasas. There still exists, on the wall of an eastern Missouri cave, a foot long (about 30 cm) drawing of the "Uktena," or horned under-water spirit, which has been very tenuously linked to the Piasa. It is a crudely drawn, limbless, slug-like creature with raccoon eyes, triangular teeth, and deer antlers. This Uktena painting has been carbon dated to 1050 AD[13]—six centuries before Marquette's expeditions. That date is typical to Mississippian-era art. Drawings from this period have only survived in caves and other sheltered environments—Midwestern weather. Therefore, it is extremely unlikely that Marquette's Piasa would date to that era. It must have been created centuries before.

---

[13] Carol Dias-Granados and James R. Duncan, *THE PETROGLYPHS of MISSOURI* (Tuscaloosa and London: The University of Alabama Press, 2000), p.42

Chasing Dragons

Some have associated the Piasa with depictions of the *Aramipichia* ("underwater panther"), the *Uktena*, or the *Manitou* (a spirit creature), three mythological creatures feared and *respected* by Native Americans.

The Aramipichia, or water panther, was depicted in many variant forms by tribes in the central United States. It was an underwater creature that attacked those who unwarily entered the water. Depictions of it are crudely drawn, and vary greatly in form. Recently, it has been suggested that water panthers might have been bull sharks. They have been known to attack humans in fresh water, and have been caught in fishermen's nets in several locations along the Illinois banks of the Mississippi River.

The *Uktena* is the Cherokee version of the water panther. However, as the Cherokee lived far to the Southeast of the Illinois Piasa, the Uktena theory is most unlikely. Also, the *Uktena* had a rattlesnake's rattle on its tail, and lacked claws.

The Manitou spirit creature has been depicted as having a human form with large, many pronged antlers.

Aside from having horns or claws, these small, crudely carved figures bear little resemblance to Marquette's Piasa. It is probable that these entities have been linked to the Piasa simply because their attributes have become confused and mingled over the centuries.

Lastly, the volume of gunfire that was directed at the Piasa clearly demonstrates that the local Native Americans feared and hated the Piasa. It was not venerated, as were the sacred petroglyphs and pictographs that *they* created.

In summary, the Piasa, as first described by Father Marquette, was virtually identical to the Imperial Chinese lóng. Lewis' 1854 painting shows a deteriorated *lóng* motif that was executed on a massive scale. The preparation of this site required excavation with metal tools, skilled carving, and painting techniques unknown to the local Native Americans or Europeans. The Illinois tribe, the local Native Americans, made no claim to the Piasa, attributing its construction to small beings from the Mississippi River. The Piasa was alien to them and greatly feared.

We believe the weight of evidence clearly points to a Chinese origin for the Piasa.

Others have uncovered much evidence that Zheng He's fleets sailed around the world. The Piasa is evidence that his men reached the banks of the mighty Mississippi. They proclaimed their great achievement by executing a towering *lóng*, carved in stone and painted in Imperial colors. It proclaimed the greatness of China to that uttermost corner of the earth.

"This concludes my remarks, thank you."

There was a moment of silence…

And then, the applause began. It was not lengthy applause, but politely enthusiastic, considerably more so than for any other report we had sat through.

The photographers that had waited so long at the back of the room now snapped pictures of everyone and everything connected to our report and then vanished. It was then that we were certain—they were there for us.

I found myself speaking to a distinguished gentleman who was carefully examining Laurie's artistic interpretation of the Piasa. He was taller than most of the Chinese we had met, with the upright and self-assured bearing of a career military man. It was no surprise then, when he introduced himself to us as Zheng Ming. Mr. Zheng was a retired Rear Admiral, and a friend of Gavin Menzies. The surprise came when he became openly emotional as we gave him a disc copy of our presentation.

In the course of our adventure, we had experienced damage to our luggage, numerous technical difficulties with an unfamiliar laptop that did not "speak" English, and had committed embarrassing but innocent blunders in etiquette. Yet, for all that, the amateur scholars from America had apparently impressed their Chinese hosts.

Two days later, we were back in the United States, at LAX, waiting for our next flight. We sat by a newlywed Chinese couple, who had returned to the States on the same flight as ours after visiting relatives in China. The young man began talking about those Americans who had just caused some excitement in Nanjing. He said they had spoken about the Chinese discovering America. There had been some celebration in the streets, he went on, and the Americans could have had the keys to the city, if they had but asked.

That was the moment it all sank in.

We had been in a cocoon and knew nothing of the enthusiastic reaction in the streets. We had seen television cameras as we began our presentation, but we had not realized that they were focused solely on us. But all glory is fleeting; when we arrived home the local papers had absolutely no interest in covering our story. Columbus had discovered America, and if there was evidence to the contrary, they simply *did not want to know*!

After returning from Nanjing, we took a brief break, and then continued to search for evidence supporting a Chinese origin for the Piasa. It has taken several years, but we have found many more pieces of the puzzle.

Mark Nickless & Laurie Bonner-Nickless

CHAPTER V

SEMPLE THE DESTROYER

Henry Lewis painted "Der Piasa Felsen" in 1846. It was first printed in 1854, as a color lithograph, in Dusseldorf, Germany. It was included, along with a series of twenty essays written by Lewis and others, to extol the virtues of the exotic Mississippi Valley and entice readers (very successfully) to emigrate from Germany to the heart of the American continent. These essays and some eighty of Lewis' paintings were compiled into a single book, *Das Illustrirte Mississippithal*.

Strangely, the destruction of the Piasa occurred nearly simultaneous with that publication.

Was this an unfortunate coincidence?

There was something very odd about the supposed reason behind its destruction. The Piasa, a source of wonderment to generations of Native Americans and Whites alike, was quarried and used as building stone or burned to produce lime for cement. Those basic materials were then used to construct the village of Elsah. The question arises—why was the Piasa destroyed for such mundane purposes when otherwise untouched limestone was abundantly available, in the form of the limestone bluffs that extended for miles north and south along the Mississippi?

Was there no respect for the ancient ones who created it?

Another question arises from the strange comment of that Elsah resident when Jim Kennedy, Bill Wu and I visited in April, 2005...

"They were giving it away..." He had marveled, referring to the lot upon which his house was built.

Who would give away free land, when Elsah was supposedly a for-profit real-estate development? It made no sense. What business-man would do something so self-defeating, so *unprofitable*?

As it turned out, the answer was Semple.

No, not simple ...Semple.

James Semple was one of the most distinguished and successful citizens of Illinois in the mid-19th century. In his lifetime, Semple was a lawyer, a brigadier-general in the Black Hawk War,[14] the ambassador to Columbia, an Illinois Supreme Court judge, inventor, a confidante of President Lincoln (who hung a portrait of Semple in his office), and eventually a United States Senator. During his time in the Senate, Semple was possibly the fiercest advocate for the expansion of the United States into the Oregon Territory along the Pacific coast. He was a true believer in the principle of Manifest Destiny. The United States had the right, he righteously proclaimed, "as clear as the noonday sun" to all territories in the North American continent from Maine to Oregon. This ex-general, who had never fired a shot in anger, was willing to wage war with England over lands along the disputed northwestern border with Canada. "54-40 or fight!" was Senator Semple's battle cry. But war was not necessary; cooler heads negotiated the Oregon Treaty.

In 1847, after his term in the Senate expired, Semple returned home to Illinois. There, he found a powerful affront to his vision of America's Manifest Destiny. Henry Lewis had recently visited the Piasa and had published a faithful painting of it in his *Das Illustrirte Mississippithal*.

The Mississippi steamboat was in its heyday, and thousands of people now traveled up and down the great river. The Piasa, albeit in a deteriorated condition, had been seen by thousands of people, and many theories were being actively voiced about its origin.

And earlier, some had a very good idea of the Piasa's origin. A 1753 Royal French map, drawn by Phillippe Bauche, identified the west coast of North America, above California, as *Fusang of the*

---

14 In 1832, a brief rebellion by the Sauk and Fox tribes in Wisconsin and Illinois, led by Chief Blackhawk.

Chinese[15]. The basis for this unusual labeling was the discovery of the account of the voyage of Hui Shen, an early sixth century Buddhist monk. Hui Shen had visited a strange land, far to the east, on the far side of the Pacific Ocean. After many years there, he returned to China and reported to the Emperor. The belief that the Chinese had visited America before Columbus was firmly fixed in the *French* mind.

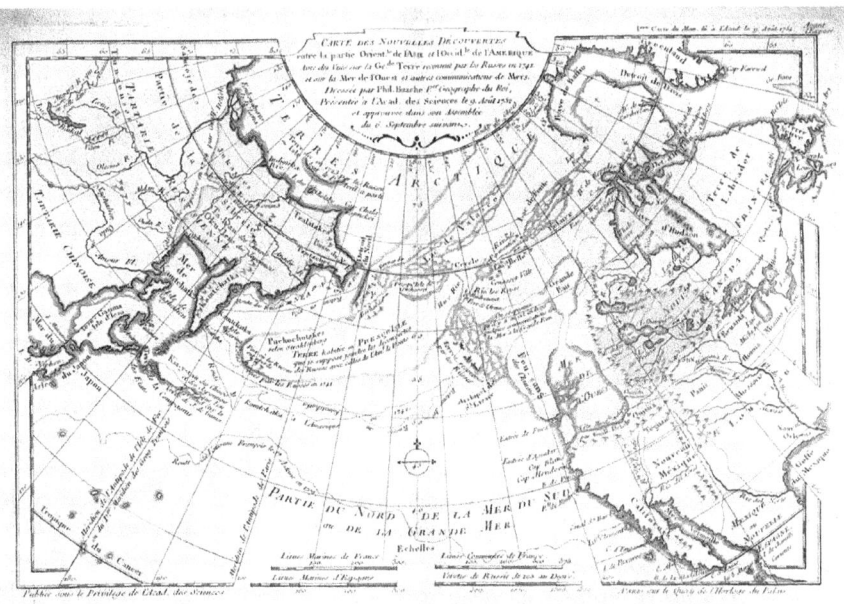

1753 BAUCHE MAP

Joseph Nicolas Nicollet would certainly have been familiar with this map. Nicollet was a Professor of Mathematics at the prestigious Lycee Louis-de-Grande in Paris, and had been a student of Bauche. He immigrated to America in 1832 for financial reasons, and in 1838-39, mapped the upper Mississippi and Missouri Valleys for the American Army.

---

[15] https://www.ancient-origins.net/artifacts-other-artifacts/buache-map-controversial-map-shows-antarctica-without-ice-005647

Chasing Dragons

An examination of a map Nicollet prepared reveals that he had faithfully mapped Piasa Creek. Therefore, he certainly saw the Piasa, which was just north of this small stream. Because of his intimate knowledge of Bauche's map, Nicollet would have concluded that the Piasa was evidence of Hui Shen's visit. He would have been wrong about *which* visit, as he knew nothing of Zheng He's 15th century visit, but he would have correctly concluded that the Piasa was evidence of a deep Chinese penetration into North America. We can imagine Nicollet's excitement as he first pointed out the Piasa to his able assistant, John C. Fremont.

John C. Fremont later gained fame as a noted explorer of the American West. His fame propelled him into politics and in 1850 he became the first Senator from the newly organized state of California. Fremont's wife was Jesse Benton, daughter of Missouri Senator Thomas Hart Benton. Senator Benton, like the Piasa's eventual destroyer, Senator Semple, was a strong proponent of Manifest Destiny. So, through this family connection, Jesse's father, Semple, and other proponents of Manifest Destiny would have learned of the Piasa's probable Chinese origin through John C. Fremont.

This revelation would have come as a shock.

This was an age of rising Sinophobia, and increasingly restrictive laws against Chinese immigration into the rich gold fields of California. It is easy to imagine Senator Semple's fury when he heard of such speculation. If Columbus had not been the first to touch upon American shores, then China could potentially lay claim to the American West by right of prior discovery! How then could America fulfill its Manifest Destiny and expand from sea to shining sea? The Piasa, symbol of that inconvenient claim, had to be suppressed. From the evidence presented here we conclude that Senator Sample applied his considerable talents to this thorny problem and came up with an answer:

Destroy the evidence.

Senator James Semple knew real estate. In 1852, he had purchased a riverfront property, known then as the Jersey Landing.

This included the Piasa and the relatively narrow, spring-fed valley immediately to its south that interrupted the bluffs overlooking the Mississippi. In 1853, Semple had that property surveyed, and then he renamed Jersey Landing, *Elsah*, a misspelling of Ailsa Rock, the last of Scotland seen by his departing ancestors.

The pieces were in place for a *profitable* land development.

Then, James Semple did something unusual for an astute businessman. He did something very *unprofitable*. He ran this unusual advertisement in the February 18, 1854 *Alton Daily Telegraph:*

> "Anyone who *builds* a house, such as may be required—and it need not be very costly — will be entitled to a *deed* for the lot on which it stands, as a donation."

Nearly free land! Just walk north a few hundred feet along the river, pick up building stone quarried from the Piasa site, lay a foundation, and a property deed would be yours!

In the next few months, the foundations for some half-dozen houses were laid. This was after the St. Louis typhoid epidemic of 1849 that killed 10% of the city's population. Survivors with money were moving out of the city and buying nearby land for new homes. It was a seller's market and Semple could have made a killing, but he chose not to.

Then, in 1857, Semple reversed himself. With his wife Mary, he organized the Elsah Building and Manufacturing Company. It *sold* lots. That turnabout made perfect sense, if the purpose of the land give-away had been to quickly destroy the Piasa by converting it into building materials. There is additional evidence to support this conclusion. On March 12, 1924, the *Alton Daily Telegraph* published a piece stating that the Piasa was most likely demolished in 1856. This date fits squarely in the middle of Semple's 1854-1857 land give-away. Mission accomplished. In 1857, it was time to recoup their losses. Within a few years, Elsah was an orderly little village of solidly built limestone cottages. And, the Piasa, survivor of "ten thousand bullets" and four centuries of exposure to the bitter elements, was no more. Just imagine the disappointment of the boat loads of freshly-arrived German immigrants, eager to see for themselves the great wonder from Lewis' book …

"Nothing to see here, Volks!"

CHAPTER VI

MANIFESTED AS AN ABSENCE

After Marquette, the next expedition exploring the Mississippi Valley was commanded by Sieur LaSalle in 1682[16]. A member of his party was Nicolas LaSalle (no relation), whose journal has been recently discovered. Nicolas recorded that the expedition voyaged down the Illinois River and arrived at its junction with the Mississippi River in February 6, 1682. They found that they could not enter the Mississippi because of "drift-ice". They camped for twelve days, awaiting better conditions. This was twelve days under the very noses of Marquette's "monsters". And what did Nicolas report? Absolutely nothing; not a word. On the face of it, this is impossible and had to have been deliberate. The entire party could not have failed to marvel at the sight.

But after this glaring lack of observation, LaSalle made an incredible statement two weeks later when they arrived at the Mississippi's junction with the Ohio River. "...This river, which comes from the Iroquois country, had caused some to believe that, in following it one might find a *passage* to China..." This is an incredible statement. How could one travel northeast, up the Ohio River toward your starting point and find a route to China?

Interestingly, in a footnote the English translator states that the original French word, *paysage* is better translated as *countryside*, but insisted on *passage* simply because a French historian had changed the word centuries ago. We had a native French speaker

---

[16] Nicolas de La Salle, *THE LA SALLE EXPEDITION ON THE MISSISSIPPI RIVER, 1682.* Edited by William C. Foster. Translated by Johanna L. Warren: Texas State Historical Association, 2003.

independently translate the section from a copy of the original manuscript. He translated *paysage* as a landmark or scenery; an indication the Chinese had been there.

It would seem that Nicolas had China on his mind. Perhaps he could not speak directly of the Piasa but found a way to hint at its existence. This Chinese monument was exceedingly inconvenient, as the whole point of the expedition was to claim the Mississippi for France. *Sieur* LaSalle claimed the Mississippi Valley for France a few weeks later.

In 1687, explorer Henri Joutel *did* see the Piasa. Joutel's journal denigrates what Marquette recorded.[17] The Piasa consisted of two crudely drawn red figures of small size. Yet Joutel admits that that the Natives paid respect to the figures. We know from Lewis' 19th century painting and other descriptions that the Piasa was neither crude nor small. Joutel was concealing what he actually witnessed.

Next in was a Franciscan missionary and explorer, Louis Hennepin[18]. He followed Sieur La Salle's route down the Illinois River to its junction with the Mississippi, where the Piasa overlooked the Father of Waters, then he turned north to find its source. His report made no mention of the Piasa. His 1698 map shows the Illinois River adjacent to Cap St. Antoine, when in fact this point is nearly a week's voyage to the south. Conveniently, with the majestic miles-long bluffs of the Mississippi missing from the Hennepin's map, there was no place for the Piasa to *be*. Hennepin even placed the mouth of the Missouri River *north* of the Illinois' junction with the Mississippi, further muddying the waters.

Were these errors deliberate?

After Hennepin, a Jesuit priest, St. Cosme, entered the Mississippi from the Illinois River on December 6, 1698. In his narrative of the voyage[19], St. Cosme mentions beautiful islands at the junction of the two rivers, yet, like Hennepin, he made no

---

[17] Ibid
[18] https://www.accessible-archives.com/2013/08/1698-friar-hennepin-map/
[19] *THE VOYAGE OF ST. COSME*, http://www.americanjourneys.org/aj-055/

mention of the Piasa painting nor the massive miles-long bluff that towered over his tiny canoes. Only after a further *downstream* voyage of some twenty miles did he describe seeing a few small rock paintings below the junction with Missouri River, on the left bank. These rock paintings would have been very small indeed, as the river bluffs had petered out several miles upstream and nothing larger than an odd boulder was available to paint on. The towering Piasa could not possibly have been there.

Six days later, and much further south, St. Cosme arrived at a bend on the Illinois side of the Mississippi River, later named Cap St. Antoine. A little way below this point, St. Cosme described a hundred-foot-tall bluff, on the Missouri side, which jutted out into the Mississippi and so caused a dangerous whirlpool. St. Cosme wrote "On one occasion fourteen Miamis perished there. This has caused the spot to be dread by the savages, who are in the habit of offering sacrifices to that rock when they pass there. We saw none of the figures that we were told we should find there." This has elements of some Piasa stories, especially concerning the sacrifices, but the location is about a hundred miles off.

It is very odd that St. Cosme saw nothing of the Piasa where we know it was located, yet claimed he was looking for "figures" six days later. Was St. Cosme's account deliberate misdirection? He made at least two statements that were true; he saw beautiful islands at the Illinois-Mississippi junction and later did *not* see any painted figures downstream at Cap St. Antoine. And perhaps he did see a few small painted figures in between. But in all these true statements there is hidden a lie; he reported nothing about the Piasa painting yet he could not possibly have missed it.

It is an amazing coincidence that Hennepin, La Salle, Joutel and St. Cosme, men of intelligence and possessing missionary zeal, each, in their turn, sailed right under the Piasa, but like Sergeant Schultz from the Sixties sitcom *Hogan's Heroes*, they had somehow seen *nothing, nothing* of the two giant dragons staring down upon them. We believe that what we have here could best be described as *evidence by absence*.

Chasing Dragons

A possible reference to the Piasa appeared on a 1717 French map[20]. A location just south of the junction of the Illinois and Mississippi Rivers is marked "Chateaux Ruines". Could this be a reference to the Piasa, or the first description of nearby Cahokia Mounds? After this enigmatic map reference, nothing in our historical records mentions the Piasa for over a century.

Lewis and Clark are justly famous for their fabled expedition. Before setting out for parts unknown, they made camp along the Mississippi at present day Wood River, Illinois. From November 1803 to March 1804 they awaited spring. Their journal goes into great detail, describing the hunts and adventures of each day. Yet nowhere does it mention the Piasa. Yet it was an elephant, err ... dragon, sitting in their living room...for months. There can be little doubt that Lewis and Clark were aware of the Piasa. On their way to their winter grounds, November 28, 1803, Lewis and Clark presented their orders to Captain Amos Stoddard. Stoddard commanded an artillery unit stationed at Kaskaskia, Illinois, south of St. Louis. The following spring, March 9, they met with Stoddard again in St. Louis for ceremonies and an inspection tour.

This is the same Captain Stoddard who later described the damage inflicted on the Piasa by "ten thousand bullets". He knew all about the beastly painting, as we suspect did everyone else in the vicinity of St. Louis.

It is difficult to believe that President Thomas Jefferson, who possessed one of the most inquisitive minds in history, would have been unaware of the 1753 Bauche map. Perhaps, things unspoken explain why one of the Lewis and Clark expedition's chief goals was to establish a route to China.

---

[20] https://www.loc.gov/item/gm71002183/

Mark Nickless & Laurie Bonner-Nickless

CHAPTER VII

THE INSCRIPTION ON FORT HILL

But other than the Piasa and the fall of Cahokia's civilization, did the Chinese leave behind any other traces of their expeditions? This question was near the top of our to-do list after we returned from Nanjing. A clue to this mystery was already in our hands, but still awaiting its proper time to be revealed. While preparing for our Nanjing trip, we had purchased a copy of *The Petroglyphs and Pictographs of Missouri*, by Carol Diaz-Granados and James R. Duncan. The book had provided some useful background information on Native American techniques for cutting and painting stone, which we had used in our paper. But, none of its images appeared to be remotely Chinese. However, in the bibliography I had recognized the name of someone I knew, so I made a mental note to contact him after our return home.

Larry Wegmann was listed as the author of a 1980 paper titled *Archaeoastonomic Sites in Jefferson County, Missouri*. Larry had done his student teaching in biology at Crystal City High School in 1968, and I had been one of his students. (Some *forty years* later, I can distinctly remember a trick question on one of his tests. I had my suspicions about it, but outsmarted myself with an overly complicated answer and missed it anyway. Ouch!)

Larry had developed an interest in local archaeology when he was introduced, by his academic adviser, to Frank Magre, an acknowledged expert in the culture and archaeology of Missouri's native peoples. Magre had graduated from Crystal City High School in 1926, after serving as class president for all four years. He was a short, energetic man with a passion for the archaeology of Jefferson and Washington Counties in Missouri. In 1991, despite his amateur status, Magre posthumously received national recognition for his studies of petroglyphs and pictographs from the American Rock Art Research Association. He was widely known for his informative and

Chasing Dragons

competently presented slideshows.

One such presentation hooked Larry, who then worked with Frank off and on for the next twenty years, recording dozens of petroglyphs, many of which have since been erased by weather and 'civilization.' In turn, Larry made use of this store of knowledge to develop insights into Native American astronomy, and how they had recorded it in stone. He eventually wrote a paper on the subject, which was quickly rejected by the conservative archaeological community. Yet, ironically, bits of this 'rejected' paper found their way, years later, into a definitive book on Missouri's Indian rock carvings!

I was unaware of any of this. I simply saw Larry's name in Diaz-Granados' book's bibliography and realized that he could be a valuable resource, especially if he was still living in the area. Fortunately, his name was in the local phone book, and he lived only 10 miles away. And so I soon found myself sitting at Larry's kitchen table, telling him about our unlikely adventure in Nanjing and the Piasa paper that had taken us there. To my relief, and perhaps because of his unhappy experience with the "Establishment," Larry did not immediately reject my story. We conversed a while, then he suddenly remembered a photograph that he wanted me to see. He could not find it immediately, so I gave him our email address before departing.

A few hours later, Laurie began downloading the photograph. She let out a gasp even before it was finished, she had immediately

recognized a Chinese character – 同 (TÓNG) – carved deeply into stone. When the download was complete, a second character could be seen, carved beside the first, but sadly, its identity was unclear.

Translating the Chinese language is often very imprecise, so we passed the photograph on to native speakers of Mandarin that we knew for their opinions, as did Larry. He was astounded when an ex-student, a young lady from Canton, China, read it effortlessly as "Love is here."

Among our sources, there was a general agreement as to what it said—"sharing love"—well sums up their various interpretations.

Sometime around 1956, after one of his slide shows, Frank Magre was told about a strange stone carving on Fort Hill, five miles north of Hillsboro, Missouri. Fort Hill had been so named because of the Union entrenchment that was hurriedly dug there in 1864 to protect St. Louis from an imminent attack. Confederate General Sterling Price had threatened St. Louis after the retreat of Union General Thomas Ewing's outnumbered garrison following the battle of Pilot Knob in Southeastern Missouri. Fortunately for St. Louis, General Price's army veered west and was eventually destroyed near Kansas City.

When he visited the Fort Hill site, Magre found an inscription that was unlike any of the other Mississippian petroglyphs he had cataloged. This inscription was carved into the wall of a rock shelter, about five feet above the ground. It was about fifteen by eight inches in size.[21]

In 1971, Magre teamed up with Brother Benjamin Ellis, a Benedictine monk. The pair of them photographed this unique petroglyph and mapped that general area. In 1978, Larry made the last known photograph of it. The inscription then caused a considerable stir among epigraphers—those that study ancient inscriptions. It was generally agreed that the carving was written language. Some speculated that it had been written in a European or North African script of some sort.

Ogam? Runic? Punic?

Professor Barry Fell, an invertebrate biologist at Harvard, and

---

21 Approximately, 38 cm by 20 cm.

amateur epigrapher, had gone so far as to declare that it was written in "Libyan," and told of buried treasure. Soon, he promised, he would make an important announcement about its meaning—an announcement that never came. Professor Fell's silence spoke volumes.

It turns out that this professor, like Russell before him, was pursuing a personal agenda; and that was to prove that "the white race" had explored America thousands of years ago. An ancient Chinese inscription in America could never be admitted to having been found, or spoken of, if it was.

With Professor Fell's misleading emphasis on a "Libyan" origin, it never entered anyone's mind to look to the East. And so, the mysterious petroglyph, which would make sense to any literate Chinese, was never deciphered by scholars.

Even so, this petroglyph was considered so important that it became a central reason for the purchase of the property it was on, by the Mastodon Park citizen's committee. This organization was led by Dorothy Heinze,[22] a friend of Frank Magre.

The land surrounding the inscription eventually became the Sandy Creek Covered Bridge Historic Site, now owned by the state of Missouri. They hoped to protect the inscription, and nearby petroglyphs that were clearly made by Native Americans. Vandals had destroyed petroglyphs before, and there was a boys' camp nearby.

As an added precaution, a latex mold was made of it, and this was sent to Professor Fell for safekeeping. Not surprisingly, given the Professor's personal agenda, this has since been lost to history. But worse was yet to come.

In 2010 and again in early 2011, Larry, Laurie and I repeatedly searched for the inscription site deep in the Ozark hills. Despite careful search during the first two trips, we did not find it where we expected, along the base of a small bluff that held several Indian

---

[22] Heinze's organization also helped create Mastodon State Park at Imperial, Missouri. Mastodon bones have been found here, one of them with a Clovis point embedded in it – a very important find.

shelters and well-worn petroglyphs. On our third attempt, we used an old map I had found among a collection of Frank Magre's papers in the archives of Hillsboro's Jefferson College. This map showed the inscription's precise location on another bluff only a few hundred yards beyond where we searched previously. This time, we found what *remained* of the carving. So much of the original sandstone had crumbled away that only one short horizontal line still survived.

Larry later realized that the acetic acid based rubber latex, poured into the inscription to make the mold, must have eaten into the sandstone, causing it to deteriorate rapidly.

Some months previously, after our first conversation, Larry had contacted Gavin Menzies. His photograph of the Fort Hill Inscription was posted on Menzies' *1421* website. It has elicited numerous responses, but one in particular stands out. It came from Dr. Michael Howatt, the author of several books on Chinese characters:

> Regarding the characters; they are 100% Chinese characters. The author (stone mason) was limited as he had only a straight cutting blade to use.
> The character on the right is 同 (*tong,* "same"). The character on the left may be incomplete or drawn by a person with poor skill, it has components of (度, *dù,* "degree, extent") and (受 , *shòu,* "receive")....

Later, after a careful study of the 76,000-character database he had compiled, Michael found an obscure character that he thought was the most likely to be the more eroded left-hand character in the inscription. That character was *"ning"*, peaceful. So, the most likely characters for the inscription read *"tong ning"*, "peaceful same", or "peaceful group":

Chasing Dragons

In Missouri's ancient St. Francois mountain range, two adjacent unique mountains, Pilot Knob and Iron Mountain, are principally composed of many millions of tons of magnetite[23] and hematite. A Union fort was built at the foot of Pilot Knob during the American Civil War to protect access to that precious resource. There, a thousand Confederate soldiers were shot down in fifteen minutes on one bloody day in 1864. This was the same battle that would lead to the digging of Union entrenchments on Fort Hill.

Those two mountains lie approximately 100 miles south of Cahokia. Take a map, draw a line from Cahokia to them. Then, find its *midpoint*; you will find it falls at a point five miles north of Hillsboro, Missouri, precisely where the inscription was carved, along a well-established Indian trail.

Indians revered the Fort Hill site. Looking through his records, Larry found a 1977 transcript of the recollections of 89-year-old Ed Johnston, who had lived in a farmhouse on Fort Hill as a young child. Mr. Johnston told of the Indians who visited Fort Hill in the early 19th century:

> It was about 1840 that the last Indians settled up there. I don't know what tribe they were but they came in here from Oklahoma looking for landmarks....My grandfather bought land that took in part of Fort Hill and he lived there. Landmarks were treasure that they had buried. You see, white men would hardly notice an Indian's landmark... Later, there was another Indian who came in here...and was here about a week...he was looking

---

23 This magnetite is an ore so rich in iron that it was once forged into useful items without refining. Iron was in short supply in Ming-dynasty China, and so highly prized.

for landmarks.

Traveling by foot or horseback several hundred miles through the rugged Ozarks would have been a grueling journey. Yet these Native Americans, most likely members of the Osage tribe, were making pilgrimages to Fort Hill as late as the 1840s, clearly looking for something very important to them. An Indian's treasure would not have been gold or silver, like a white man's. It would have been something of spiritual or historical significance. A landmark perhaps, commemorating some powerful event.

Surely, something very important happened at Fort Hill.

CHAPTER VIII

WHENCE WINGS?

Father Marquette clearly described two creatures without wings. Yet in later accounts these appendages sometimes appeared, and sometimes they did not. Spencer Russell, the honest son of Professor Russell (he admitted that his father sometimes made things up) made this observation around 1849:

> I used to climb the rocks to look at it when I was a boy. I have been within sixty feet of it. I once pointed it out from the deck of an English steamer to a lady and she looked at it from a field glass. No wings showed that day for the weather was dry. The colors were always affected by dampness, and stood out distinctly after rain. Father Marquette evidently saw the Piasa on a dry day for he pictured it without wings. The picture was cut into the rock a half an inch or more, and originally painted with red, black, and blue. It had the head of a bear, large, dis-proportioned teeth, and the horns of an elk, the scaly body of a fish and a bear's legs, ending in eagle's claws. The tail was at least fifty feet long, and wound three times around the body, and ended in a spearhead. The upper horns were painted red, and the lower portions and the head black. The wings were extended to the right and left of the face, and the Piasa was at least sixteen long. Its head and neck were covered with mane and its body confusedly colored with the three colors used. (Interview with Mary Hartwell Catherwood)

Most of the once vivid colors of this Ming qilin have faded until only blue remains.

This mystery of the "wings" that were seen only under wet conditions can be easily explained—*if* the artists used glassy cobalt-based paints as we posited in our original Nanjing paper—a paint pigment unknown in the west until the early 19th century. According to the younger Russell, the wings were on either side of the "face" which can be seen at the lower center of Lewis' painting. That face looks like a child's work. It is an oval with dashes for its mouth and eyes; and a spot for its nose. It is partially encircled by *feathers* which begin under its chin. It is the sort of image produced by a three year-old who draws her mother as a face and limbs without a body. The impression one gets is that someone climbed up a ladder and crudely painted a face over something previously there—in short, vandalism. It is surely not the work of artists "as good as any in Europe," as Marquette had observed.

Chasing Dragons

We have traced the basic elements of the Piasa that are found in Henry Lewis' painting. Lewis executed his painting just two or three years before the younger Russell made his observations. The Piasa had degenerated to the point that Marquette's two monsters clearly were seen as one seemingly disjoined creature. A careful side-by side comparison of our sketch with a line drawing of the Nanjing Memorial[24] reveals the origin of the fabled wings and other features that have confused researchers and the public for generations.

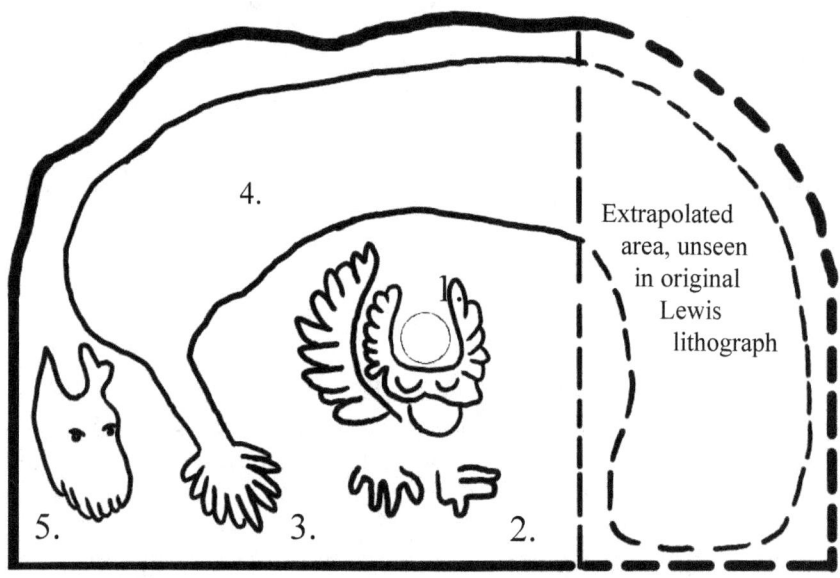

We have removed the dashes that comprise the "smiley face" at (1) on the sketch. These were obviously drawn by vandals, or would-be restorers. After this cleanup a different "face" emerges. It is adorned by two antlers with a "wing" on the left, as was described by Spencer Russell.

---

24 The Nanjing memorial was erected by Zheng He's surviving sailors upon their return to China after the 1433-34 voyages to America. It is clearly nothing less than the Piasa painting projected into three dimensions.

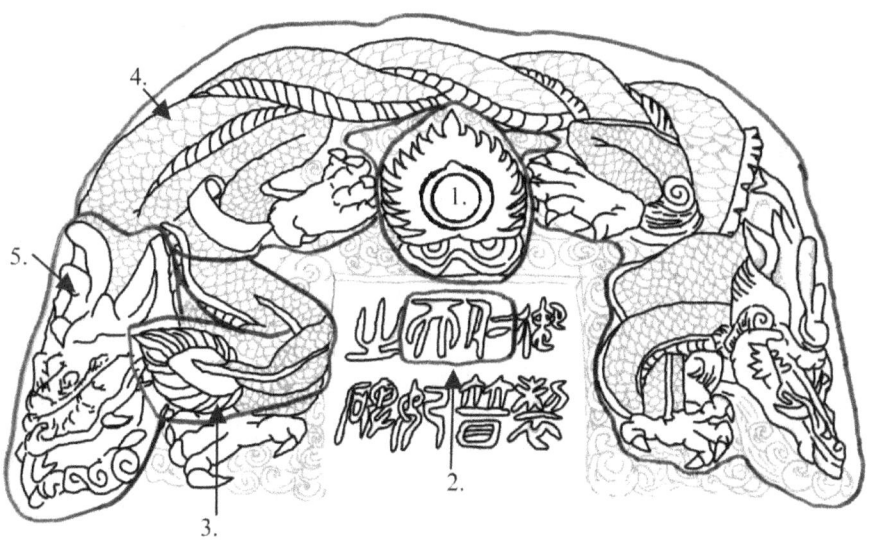

This same feature (1) is clearly visible in the center of the Nanjing Memorial. There it is much more distinct and can be immediately recognized for what it is. It is a *pearl*—specifically, the legendary luminous pearl—so important in Chinese symbolism, and it is surrounded by a corona of flames. This feature of the Nanjing Memorial can easily be transformed to resemble the Piasa's face and wings. Erase the top of the flames and the pearl vanishes. The corona then becomes a set of horns, or wings, or both, depending upon the mindset of the observer.

With the addition of a few crude dashes in the sconce upon which the pearl rests, a nose and two eyes are produced. The precious pearl and its encircling flames have become the winged face painted by Lewis. The feet of the Piasa (2) are revealed to be seal characters that have simply deteriorated. The feathery tail (3) to the lower left of the central pearl is part of the fifty-foot long tail (Spencer Russell's estimate) of a dragon.

Chasing Dragons

***NANJING MEMORIAL TO THE FINAL VOYAGE
OF THE MING TREASURE FLEET[25]***

The tail in Nanjing is positioned somewhat differently. But notice that in this three-dimensional carving, the dragon heads have been turned to face outward, leaving more room for the tail. This head position would not work so well in the two-dimensional Piasa. The absurdly large wings which appeared in the late 19th century portrayals of the Piasa, are easily explained once the deterioration of the painting is factored in. The Piasa of the early 19th century possessed what appeared to be small wings around a central face. The "wings," outlined in cobalt-based paint that shined and stood out when wet, were actually weathered flames surrounding the central pearl.

Over time, as the Piasa continued to deteriorate through

---

25 This is the photograph Laurie unwittingly took in the Temple of Kwan Yin. (Temple exterior can be seen at right)

weathering and vandalism, these small wings became less distinct and eventually faded from view. At some point, the public began to perceive the rough arc of light-colored limestone (4), which originally was the two entwined bodies, as wings.

The horned, dragon-like face (5) at the lower left obviously corresponds to the dragon head in the Nanjing Memorial. It is now clear that Marquette's two monsters, faithfully recorded by Lewis, were nothing less than a deteriorated, vandalized, traditional two-headed Chinese "*sheng*" or "*rainbow dragon*."

Chasing Dragons

In 1887, a new image of the Piasa appeared in *The Devil Among The Indians, or Record of Ancient Races in the Mississippi Valley*, written by William McAdams. According to McAdams' daughter, it was based on old testimony, which would be pre-1857. It was not drawn by a firsthand witness. This new Piasa is an amalgamation of grossly exaggerated features. The wings are huge. The tail is incredibly long and thin. Huge antlers and a long flowing beard adorn an incredibly demonic human face. In short, it is a monstrosity, drawn by someone who had never seen the original in all its glory, but who had, perhaps, heard the tall tales. The two great monsters witnessed by Marquette in 1673 had become an abominable *bearded bird*. The great dragons were lost to history – *until now*.

CHAPTER IX

REMNANTS OF MEMORY

Surely, the natives of this region would have enthralled their children and grandchildren with tales about strange visitors. Have any memories of such a visit survived? It seems so. The Osage believe their ancestors built the mounds of Cahokia. This is an odd assertion, for the Osage were once the "Lords of the Plains," a horse culture which dominated the plains far to the west of the Mississippi River and its agricultural civilization. But this was not always so. Anthropologists say that the Osage originated in the east.

There is also an Osage oral tradition, recorded by Louis F. Burns, which speaks of a westward migration and an encounter with a strange village:

> In the beginning the *Wa sha she*, *Hun ka* and *Tsi shu* lived in the Upper Worlds. Eventually they obtained bodies and souls. Then they descended to earth. After they descended they wandered over the land. The *Wa sha she* led the way, followed by the *Hun ka* and lastly the *Tsi shu*. Many years of wandering brought them to the outskirts of a strange village. As the news was passed back from the *Wa sha she* to the *Hun ka* and then to the *Tsi shu*, the strangers who heard the words, came to see who was there.
>
> Only the *Wa sha she* entered the village. The *Hun ka* and *Tsi shu* refused to enter because they were upset about the condition of the village. Bones of men and animals were scattered all over the village; a foul odor polluted the air. Men and women conducted themselves in an unbecoming manner.

Chasing Dragons

This was a village of death and disorder. The Osages were seeking life and order. As the leader of the *Wa sha she* and the leader of the strange village people sat down to talk, the *Wa sha she* leader identified himself as a *Hun ka*. The stranger raised his hand to his mouth to show his surprise. Then he said, "I am also a *Hun ka*." The strange *Hun ka* related how his people destroyed life when it appeared, using the four winds as weapons. Wherever his people directed the winds; all living things fell and died. At this time the *Wa sha she* leader invited the strange people to live with them. However, the *Wa sha she* indicated that his people did not like the habit of destroying life. He further suggested that everyone "move to a new country," where the land was pristine and free of death and disorder. The *Hun ka U ta non tse* or Isolated Earth as these strange people were called, accepted the invitation and joined the *Wa sha she*, *Hun ka*, and *Tsi shu*.

Here we have a clear description of a group of migrating Osage encountering the survivors of a catastrophic epidemic. Their village was full of dead people and animals. Notice their myth says animals, not dogs. Dogs are typically the only animal associated with Indians who lived in what would become the United States. They served as guards, beasts of burden, and sometimes food. However, early Spanish records state that the Mayans kept herds of deer in fenced areas as well as doves, turkeys and ducks.

This piece of oral history hints at how the Piasa came to be associated with terrible epidemic disease. It is not surprising that there were dead animals in the strange village the Osage stumbled upon.

In 1811, Henry Brackenridge also remarked on evidence of a great dying at Cahokia, which confirms the Osage account:

> There is, perhaps, no spot in the western country, capable of being more highly cultivated,

or of giving support to a more numerous population than this valley. If any vestige of the ancient population were to be found, this would be the place to search for it—accordingly, this tract, as also the bank of the river on the western side, exhibits proofs of an immense population. If the city of Philadelphia and its environs were deserted, there would not be more numerous traces of human existence. The great number of mounds, and the *astonishing quantity* of human bones, everywhere dug up, *or found on the surface of the ground*, with a thousand other appearances, announce that this vicinity was at one period, filled with habitations and villages. The whole face of the bluff, or hill which bounds it to the east, appears to have been a continual burial ground.[26]

Bones everywhere and exposed, on the surface? This does not sound like orderly burials. It sounds like sick people who died where they dropped and were abandoned, un-buried. It is not surprising that many bones on the surface were found along the low bluff. A sick person staggering east while attempting to flee the pestilence of the city would find even these lowly bluffs and hills an insurmountable obstacle. He or she would simply have collapsed and died.

The Osage had a custom which continually increased their numbers and their power. They were quite open to adoption of non-Osage into their tribe. In their culture, any outsiders, even entire tribes, could ceremonially become Osage, and thus join the tribe. Burns notes that the Osage experienced a population explosion as they migrated west between the 14th and 16th Centuries, "from the absorption of alien groups."

It is evident from the Osage myth that they absorbed Cahokia's

---

26 Italics mine.

survivors into their numbers.[27] In this way, the Osage of the Great Plains could claim to be the builders of the great mound complex of Cahokia.

And, there is a second tribe that perhaps has retained their own remnant of memory from the mound builder era. A few individuals in the 20th century claimed to be descendants of the Tamaroa tribe, which lived in the Cahokia area in historic times. These included Gerhardt Cappell. Mr. Cappell was interviewed in 1976, at age 89, by John K. White, director of the Native American Studies Program at Northwestern University in Illinois. Cappell recalled more than twenty words which he said were Tamaroa. This was potentially very important to linguists, as that language was believed extinct.

Linguist Carl Masthay included an examination of Gerhart Cappell's claims in his Kaskaskia Illinois-to-French Dictionary because those alleged Tamaroa words appeared to be related to known Kaskaskian words. In a lengthy essay, Masthay admitted that a circumstantial case could be made for the authenticity of Cappell's Tamaroa words, but ultimately concluded that they were most likely a fabrication. Perhaps, one perpetuated by White (who was one-quarter Cherokee), in order to help revive Indian culture in western Illinois.

Masthay had two major objections. Cappell claimed to be one-sixteenth Tamaroa. But a study of his genealogy showed his great-great grandmother, Marguerite Muret, to be half-Osage, and not Tamaroa. And, the Osage lived far to the west—wrong tribe, in the wrong place.

However, as Louis F. Burns recorded, the Osage originated in the east and slowly migrated westward through Illinois, adopting the remnants of other tribes along the way. So Marguerite's mother could have joined the Osage tribe, yet have been of Tamaroa ancestry. Most likely she would have been a member of the Isolated Earth People clan. This would not have confused an Indian familiar with Osage ways. But, this subtlety would have been lost to a white man chronicling local births and deaths in the early 19th century. To

---

27   The ancestors of the Osage clan known as the Isolated Earth people?

him, an Osage was just an Osage.

At this point, the reader might wonder why we are discussing the ancestry of one Gerhart Cappell, who lived a quiet life and died in obscurity in 1977. It is because of something he said during a discussion with White about the "Piasa bird":

> They say it wrong. You say it Pa'essa—It means 'dragon'. They lived in caves and swooped down on you when you were going along in a canoe....If you got one [coming after you?], you throw a dog in there for them or tobacco if you don't have a dog....

There is obviously a hint of Russell's flesh-eating bird story in this, but Cappell was certain the Piasa was not a bird, but a dragon. The Piasa has never been a dragon in White tradition or literature. Yet, here was an old man, of Native ancestry, asserting a contradictory view, with no motivation for doing so, unless, perhaps, it happened to be the *truth*.

CHAPTER X

CHINESE CORROBORATION: ENTER LUO MAO DENG

We know that something momentous happened to the Mississippian civilization centered at Cahokia around the time that the Piasa was constructed. A number of archaeologists have long theorized that a pandemic plague might have been the cause of Cahokia's final population crash and abandonment. Our own research, which we will discuss later, indicates that the collapse occurred around 1433 or 1434. Osage legends about their tribal origin whisper clues about this catastrophic event, but archaeologists have never identified a contagion sufficiently virulent to trigger such an event. Theories have been offered up that vary wildly from the mildly incredible to the problematic, including a contagion introduced by migratory birds. All that archaeologists can agree upon with assurance is:

> "Societies with a Mississippian level of sociopolitical organization remained alive and healthy in the deep South until the sixteenth century and the advent of European diseases to which they had no resistance. In the lower Tennessee and Ohio valleys and in the central Mississippi valley, including Cahokia, Mississippian settlements and temple towns were abandoned about 1400 leaving behind what Stephen Williams has called "the vacant quarter...."[28]

Incredibly, recent research based on chemical analysis of

---

[28] Centered on the Ohio-Mississippi River Confluence, the Vacant Quarter stretched from the American Bottom in Illinois, southward to the base of the Missouri boot heel, and up the lower Ohio River into southeast Indiana.

layers of fecal residue at the bottom of a lake adjacent to Cahokia Mounds provides scientific evidence that the city's population dropped to its nadir around 1440.[29] This is within a decade of *our* 1433/4 date for the collapse of Cahokia!

The historical record contains many accounts of pandemic plagues among Native American populations *after* the arrival of European explorers and settlers. Outbreaks of smallpox, influenza, measles, and cholera killed most Native Americans after their first contacts with Europeans.

But to date there is no explanation accepted by academia that definitively explains this widespread *pre-Columbian* population crash and the abandonment of town centers and established villages in the Middle Mississippi Valley region.

Our theory points toward a simple, logical vehicle for disease transmission—Chinese explorers. But we needed irrefutable proof to back our theory; something which we had yet to find. This has been the club which the opposition has applied to anyone who has posited that the Chinese visited America before Columbus.

Repeatedly they have demanded, "Where are the written records?"

The point is valid. How could China, inventor of bureaucracy, have completed such a voyage of discovery, then left behind no written records of it? Surely, in some obscure and dusty archive, in some forgotten corner, *something* remained after the burning of "useless records" by the Mandarin Liu Daxia of the Ming Ministry of War in 1644. This was the final blow by the Ming bureaucracy to

---

29 White, A. J. & R. Stevens, Lora & Lorenzi, Varenka & Munoz, Samuel & Lipo, Carl & Schroeder, Sissel. (2018). "An evaluation of fecal stanols as indicators of population change at Cahokia, Illinois". *Journal of Archaeological Science*. 93. 129-134. 10.1016/j.jas.2018.03.009.

Also, this paper can be read at –
https://www.researchgate.net/publication/324869183_An_evaluation_of_fecal_stanols_as_indicators_of_population_change_at_Cahokia_Illinois

erase from history the failed seventh expedition of the Great Ming Fleet. The erasure of the fleet had also begun with fire. Two centuries earlier, the surviving ships of the Treasure Fleet had been put to the torch, at anchor, after their return without their Admiral, Zheng He.

In 2006, Laurie had an "AHA!" moment, remembering something she had read weeks earlier while doing research. In Louise Levathes' *When China Ruled the Seas: The Treasure Fleet of the Dragon Throne, 1405-1433*, the author quoted at length from an obscure, *unofficial* account of Zheng He's seventh voyage. Luo Mao Deng wrote *An Account of the Western World Voyages of the San Bao Eunuch* in 1585. Once considered a work of fiction because of its supernatural elements, Luo's 100-chapter epic is now understood to have "historical value." *An Account of the Western World Voyages of the San Bao Eunuch* departs from better known Ming histories in a crucial aspect—Luo said that Zheng He sailed into the Western Ocean (i.e. the Atlantic) rather than tragically dying *en route* home in the midst of the Indian Ocean, where he was reported to have been buried at sea.[30]

In Levathes' chapter 11, "The Sultan's Bride," we came across an account of a bizarre episode from the last of that fleet's voyages. It was drawn from chapters 87-93 of Luo Mao Deng's late 16th century novel, partially translated by Anne Swann Goodrich for her book *Chinese Hells*. According to Luo, when the fleet was in the Middle East visiting Mecca—what the Chinese called Tianfang or the Celestial Quarter—Zheng He wondered what countries lay farther west. though he was warned that nothing lay beyond the western sea, he boldly continued.

The fleet sailed west for several months until the sun and stars vanished and it was impossible to navigate. For another month the

---

30 This report of Zheng He's death at sea is second-hand, and purportedly dates from 1457. However, the note with this report was not discovered until 1982, when it was found tucked into the last surviving copy of Luo's epic. Oddly, this copy had been in the hands of scholars since the time of Ann Swann-Goodrich's work – note undiscovered.

ships progressed slowly in a thick fog until land was sighted, a forbidding coast covered in snow. The admiral sent one of his officers, Wang Ming, to explore the country. Wang discovered a strange walled city in which the people had heads of oxen or horses and snakelike mouths with forked tongues and bulging eyes. It was not, however, until he met his wife—who had died ten years before—that he realized to his horror he was in the underworld....

A voyage to the Underworld?

To Laurie it sounded more like a crossing of the Atlantic Ocean to snowy Canada. And if the ocean crossing was a real event, then the city was real. Laurie excitedly realized that there was a walled city in North America whose inhabitants wore headdresses of animal heads, styled their hair like horses' manes, and held snakes in their mouths while they danced. It was Cahokia—only a few miles southeast of the Piasa.

It was an incredible theory and could only be tested in one way. Laurie was determined to find a copy of Luo's *AN ACCOUNT OF THE WESTERN WORLD VOYAGES OF THE SAN BAO EUNUCH* and see for herself.

This was a daunting, but not impossible task. She had previously translated selections from the classic *Monkey King* (*Journey to the West*) from a children's book we had purchased for our daughters at the Golden Eagle department store in Nanjing.

We called a friend who had business contacts in China. He evidently had some pull, because a few weeks later we were presented with a copy of the last fifty chapters of Luo's book. When we opened it, a business card fell out.

The name on that card was Zheng Ming. The old Admiral was looking out for us.

That was in 2006. Laurie has been working on her translation *ever since*—and her slow progress is not because of a lack of skill on her part—the Chinese themselves do not understand this book. It is written in literary Mandarin, a dialect formerly used within the confines of the Imperial court, and is full of figurative language and obscure illusions. "This way (meaning the book) leads to madness" warned Frank Lee, an associate of author Gavin Menzies.

For a while, he appeared correct.

But, Laurie has doggedly persevered with translating and her ongoing work to shed light on Luo's complete account is succeeding beyond anyone's wildest expectations.

Because of her efforts, we now know that in 1433, Admiral Zheng He and his men sailed to the Americas and visited Cahokia, which they called Fengtu. Their contact with the cultural heart of the Mississippian civilization in North America changed the course of history.

This final visit to the Americas was recorded in Luo Mao Deng's *An Account of the Western World Voyages of the San Bao Eunuch*. And, as we shall see, Luo's epic tale includes the Piasa.

Mark Nickless & Laurie Bonner-Nickless

CHAPTER XI

CHINESE CORROBORATION: THE TAOIST MASTER'S MODEST PROPOSAL

The first illustration in AN ACCOUNT OF THE WESTERN WORLD VOYAGES OF THE SAN BAO EUNUCH

In 1729, Jonathan Swift anonymously published his satirical essay titled "A Modest Proposal." Its cannibalistic suggestions were monstrous, and intended to shock the callous members of polite society in his day into mercy and compassion for poor Irish Catholics.

In the first chapter of Luo's epic, a proposal similar to Swift's sets into motion a horrific series of events, and does so with far different intentions and truly disastrous results.

In what he claimed was a "vision of the Buddha", the Taoist Celestial Master, a close spiritual adviser of the Emperor, makes a "modest" proposal that appealed to Emperor Xuande's immense ego. The Taoist Master's proposal was accepted and he was appointed as one of the leaders of the seventh and final set of voyages of the Ming Treasure Fleet. His proposal created a second mandate to be added to the one handed down by Emperor Xuande to "tell the world that I am Emperor of the entire universe."

The Taoist Master claimed he had been told by the gods themselves to deliver a very "special" gift to the savage barbarians of Fengtu.

This was a gift of "heavenly flowers" and an examination of illustration after illustration showing this Taoist leader in the text of Luo's epic depicts him carrying flowers. In the very first illustration included with Luo's text, those flowers are not only shown but are directly referenced in the vertical columns which can be seen in that illustration (included at the beginning of this chapter). The captions are arranged to be read starting first on the right side of that illustration, then moving to the smaller second one, and ending with the third column on the far left.

And, they say:
1. The sending forth of those wise and virtuous men selected by the gods from the mountain to plainly and directly offer that which must be seriously taken to heart.

2. The process of careful divination reveals the truth.

3. And by chance, in the Orchid Temple, there is an unexpected meeting for those called to carry *the harsh and unreasonable burden of the flowers* to those struggling to throw the call of the moon.

These words and images make very little sense at first glance, but from that first illustration onward, it quickly becomes clear that the Taoist Master's "heavenly flowers" cannot be actual flowers.

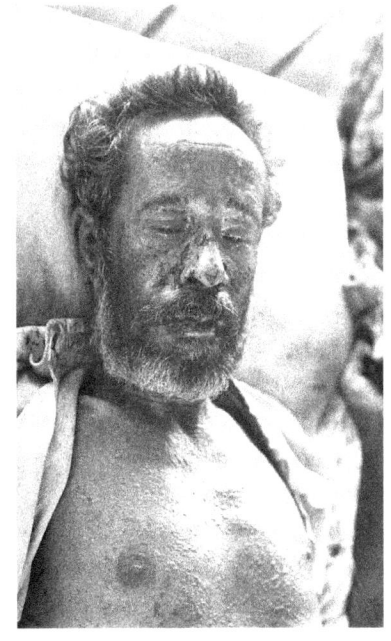

In chapter eighty-seven, soon after Wang Ming arrived in the capital of Fengtu, that advance scout for the fleet began to notice people whom he considered strange not merely for how they dressed, but for how they were horribly disfigured. They are described as "having an appearance like that of burnt firewood logs."

People who "look like burnt logs" are seldom still capable of movement and speech.

Knowing what was in the archaeological record, Laurie made a guess about what Luo really meant, and began to search through both Western and Chinese sources for evidence to support her hypothesis.

Sadly, she had guessed correctly.

Heavenly flowers was a pretty name for something darker and more deadly that also bloomed—the small red spots of smallpox. In all cases of smallpox, lesions appeared first on the face and head and were most prominent on the hands and feet of its victims. In this more common erupted form of smallpox, a minimum of 94% fatalities would have been suffered by the previously unexposed populations in and around the capital of Fengtu. Even among those who might have been fortunate enough to survive this contagion many would have either gone blind, suffered other damage to their internal organs, or have been permanently crippled by arthritic deformations of their joints.

But, the men and women with blackened faces, arms, and legs were displaying symptoms of an even more virulent form of smallpox: "black pox." In that rarer form of the contagion, which was also known as "hemorrhagic smallpox," bleeding occurred under the skin, making it appear charred and black. Typically, only appearing in 2% of all historically recorded cases, "black pox" was 100% fatal, no matter who contracted it. And, it appears that the most deadly form had spread like wildfire through the citizens of Fengtu.

At the beginning of chapter 89 of Luo's account, the urgent pleas of the people of Fengtu for justice were recorded. They begged their ruler to punish the strange visitors from China for intentionally poisoning them.

Returning to the explanation that one of the seventh group of petitioners was "a man whose terrible appearance resembled that of a log of firewood burning from within", and you could not see to judge the appearance of the hair of his head, and his hands no longer appeared like normal hands, and his feet no longer looked like normal feet. His features were sunken and oozed with pus, blackened as if scorched by fire and covered with bumps, as a matter of fact inside him an excessively fiery fever was burning, therefore it was reasonable to describe this man as one appeared to be on fire like a log.

This man wept and wailed, saying: "We are a hard-working people, who tend the crops and gather them in and bring them into the storehouses, all in all numbering 3,500 people. Because we are citizens of the Southern emperor and gather our crops at his bidding, can you give us aid? A response of five battalions and their officers must be sent by the Southern Emperor to supervise and direct our deliverance from a deadly attack upon us; the soldiers from the ships have circulated a deadly fever among all our people. The wicked men from the dragon god's empire wage war against us, how can those who have been so abundantly and intimately betrayed fight back against their poisonous treachery? We still live but even as we speak a full 3,500 of us are burning with a deadly fever. The truth of the situation is that we are without guilt in this matter, and so are requesting these five battalions and their wise commanders to come and find a way to thwart this poisonous plot and restore the natural order of our lives."

And here again, further along in the same chapter, Luo hints that one group of men are dying directly as a result of the plotting of the Taoist master and they know it:

...The twenty-second group to come forward to give their complaint was another cadre of soldiers. About half of this group appeared to have fallen ill, and the greater part of those appeared to be sinking towards their end. The sick and suffering ones wept and wailed piteously, and spoke up, saying: "We are the Xilan country's guard against attacks from military forces coming in by way of the great river, we are anxious for the Southern emperor to send out a new guard and military commander to work out what is the source of this poisonous attack that has overtaken the men of our guard and unexpectedly destroyed our strength and well-being, a calamity which is ending our lives. We stubbornly refuse go down into death of our own accord, and so declare that we will only be content with an assurance that a new guard and commander will be found and finish the task of avenging our destruction by thwarting this poisonous plot."

One of the officers over these men came forward and wept and wailed, and spoke, saying: "We are the rank and file soldiers of the Xilan country, and we are anxious for a new commander to put an end to this poisonous plot that is bringing about our deaths. One man with a sword, and only one sword has hewn down our ranks. What crime of ours merits our destruction? Charge the incoming commander and troops with finding answers and so avenging our lives."

(In another illustration from Luo shown above, the Taoist offers his "heavenly flowers" to what appears to be a more literal than realistic depiction of the "Loach King.")

And then in Chapter 96, there is an encounter with one local leader who has begun to figure out what has been done to them. A leader whose actions explain why civilization in the Southern parts of the Mississippian world would survive until the arrival of the Spanish explorers hundreds of years later:

While this conversation was as yet unfinished, all were surprised to see the Loach King come into sight, arriving on the scene while the current battle was still only half-finished. On board his vessel, at the back of the Loach King, there were scarlet banner-flags covered with fine calligraphy which was unreadable, and a fog of sacred smoke seethed around him, a foggy cloud which he sat at the discordant heart of. His was the seat of honor afforded a chieftain and head of government, and he wore the deep red robes of a monarch with full and heavy sleeves, a belt of jade, and a tall crown, and what looked to be the highest officials of his imperial court sat before him on his boat, men with the air about them of sages of great learning and virtue, and this king sat atop a throne shaped like a water lily while all of his courtiers paid him homage, bowing in submission and cupping one hand in the other before their chests, crying aloud, saying: "All here before your throne offer you their most reverent congratulations about the completion of this great endeavor!"

The Vice-admiral together with the Taoist Master, and the chief Buddhist Missionary, were shocked, however, they had no idea of how this monarch would respond to this or why these courtiers would say this, only that he replied to these men by asking: "You engage in speculating about how this will end. We exhaust ourselves but achieve nothing gathered in as a harvest. So why then do you think I should receive your fervent congratulations?"

This failed harvest appears to have been in that the epidemic was causing a shortage of human beings available to become sacrificial victims and slaves.

With sighs and groans, the court officials replied: "Messenger of the four quarters of the world, we do not seek to give insult to the lord of destiny, but it is fitting for your scholar-officials to say this! Do you mean to say that it is disrespectful to recognize an occasion for celebration when they see it?"

This appears to be a reference to the Mayans' four giant gods (Bacabs) who supported the sky. But a second possible interpretation of this is a reference to the Aztecs' four gods associated with each of the directions—Tezcatlipoca in the north, Huitzilopochtli in the south, Quetzalcoatl in the west, and Xipe Totec in the east. Tezcatlipoca was also the lord of destiny.

This debate over their next course of action between the Loach King and his chief advisers continued. When the Field marshal interjected questions of his own, the conversation took a remarkable turn as the Loach King and his companions spoke of a prior contact with China and one of its past prime ministers. A contact which the locals specifically identified as having taken place during the Song dynasty, hundreds of years before. Luo also uses this as an opportunity to subtly decry the excesses of Xuande and the disastrous results of his unchecked egotism.

The revered prince put an end to the debate by turning the attention of all concerned back to their present altercation:

"...May I dare to venture to ask the aged ministers, for what reason has such a large number of your people come here with you by boat?"

That honest government official and scribe replied: "Actually, I'm afraid that they have all traveled here in this great cadre of vessels because of the *accursed livestock* which, when left behind by explorers from your *bao chuans*, have bequeathed a legacy of suffering and death upon our people, Consequently, we returned to the long-standing practice of taking travelers into temporary custody, but merely concentrating upon keeping them from doing anything illicit in secret from the time when we deliver them safely until they are ready to depart once more."

The revered Prince asked: "How is it that this re-institution of a long-standing practice is the result of your people hearing reports about groups of explorers in smaller ships making gifts of accursed animals that brought calamity upon those who received them?"

The honest government official and scribe smiled, and explained: "It is plain that every time someone has personally received one of these gift animals from your groups of explorers, they have contracted a deadly illness, therefore, we recognized that these animals are the cause."

The revered Prince asked: "How is it that you can be certain that these animals and those who gave them are always the cause of this inheritance of suffering and death for those they come into contact with?"

The honest government official and scribe replied: "In short, those who died met a member of your expedition face to face or one of the students of your religions, it is because of this offense that our noble court, and our monarch, *Zhūyá* **(珠崖),** would subject the members of your expedition to censure, because some of those under your governing authority have engaged in giving gifts with sources of excessive harm hidden inside them to a vast number of people in the southern lands. Three days after they leave, the trap springs shut on those who make contact with that cursed livestock. Occasionally then, some of those who were present come back, but only enough to fill a single small boat, and even those only narrowly escape being among those whose villages are completely destroyed by this objective, so it is not always a fact that all of the generations living in a village fall victim to this ploy. Haven't enough suffered injury and harm because of it?"

The revered Prince declared: "From this day forward, who would dare to speak of making such trouble or dare to act to cause others so much suffering!"

As in the modern case of the spread of SARS and other diseases, livestock has repeatedly been the culprit behind the spread of pandemic diseases. This situation clearly sheds light on the mystery of why the term 宝船 (bǎo chuán) has come to not only mean the great capital ships of the Ming-dynasty (aka "treasure ships"), but also has become a Buddhist figure of speech for "the eternal salvation of the multitudes is more important than the sea of bitterness that must be endured to reach that other shore of the Dharma."

The revered prince deeply desired both to get their vessels moving again, and to ask more questions, this Loach King needed to be gotten rid of, his clouds of red banner flags needed to be dispersed and scattered one by one, the hazy mists of sacred smoke that surrounded him needed to be wafted away and brought to its end, another generation did not need to have to die to force him out of power.

The revered Lord San Bao said: "It is easy to appease the dead as well as gain the favor of the spirits of the land."

These native people of Fengtu had no prior knowledge of, and no defenses against, what the Taoist had plotted with his emperor to unleash upon them.

This plotting was done with the expectation that such an epidemic would merely disrupt their society, discredit their gods and priest kings and so encourage the people of Fengtu to cast aside their cannibalistic religious practices. The religious leaders of China were certain that the suitably humbled and penitent people of Fengtu would eagerly convert to Buddhism and Taoism instead. The Taoist master had expected his plans would also create a leaderless mass of humanity ready to hand over the vast resources of the "iron mountains" (today, the St. Francis Mountain range) as vassals ready to accept the "benevolent" rule of Xuande.

These plans directly contradicted the concept known as the "Mandate of Heaven" which can be explained simply as that the Chinese emperor acted as the "Son of Heaven" and had a valid claim to the throne only as long as he served his people well. The Mandate of Heaven held the Emperor as solely responsible for the state of the world. Among the signs that any particular ruler had lost the Mandate of Heaven were drought, famine, floods, and earthquakes. Common people were not believed to hold the same power to influence the overall state of the world and so anger the heavenly powers to the point of bringing down upon themselves and the world such natural cataclysms. The Mandate justified rebellion against an unjust, tyrannical, or incompetent ruler. Open rebellion was justified to allow heaven to take away the mandate and give it to another. And if that rebellion was successful in overthrowing a ruling dynasty, this was taken as proof that they had lost the Mandate of Heaven and the rebel leader had gained it. Unlike the hereditary Divine Right of Kings, being granted the Mandate of Heaven did not depend upon the one receiving it being of royal or even noble birth. Any successful rebel leader could become emperor with Heaven's approval, even if he was born a peasant. In this way, the Han Dynasty had been founded, and even the Mongols could have claimed this mandate as their justification in the founding their Yuan Dynasty.

Zhu Yuanzhang, who would later take the name Hongwu as the first of the Ming dynasty Emperors, had studied Confucianism during his days as a rebel leader trying to gain the approval of China's scholarly gentry. Claiming that mandate, he took up the title of Son of Heaven and established the Ming Dynasty (明朝; *Míng Cháo*) in 1368. His son Zhu Di would later invoke this mandate as justification to justify seizing the imperial throne from his nephew and making himself Emperor Yongle. Yongle's (Zhudi's) grandson would also use the mandate as justification when he claimed even higher status for himself and his heirs, and by that action brought China's ambitions for global domination crashing down around them:

> Imperial decree (by Emperor Xuande) on Zheng He's mission in *Ming Shi Lu*
>
> On the 9th day of the 6th month in the 5th year of Xuande (1430), Zheng He was dispatched to visit foreign native states. The decree is as follows:
> I obeyed the decree of heaven and inherited the throne from Emperor Taizu, Taizong, and Renzong. Being the emperor of the universe with a reign title of Xuande, I fear the foreign native states located far away are not aware of it. …

Xuande then gave further explanation of his intentions and with this an implied threat of what might happen if acceptance of his "universal" status was no enthusiastically accepted.

> …I send eunuchs Zheng He and Wang

Jinghong with this imperial order to instruct these countries to follow the way of heaven (the mandate) with reverence and to watch over their people so that all might enjoy the good fortune of lasting peace.

Add to this fit of self-aggrandizement that, during this final cycle of world-wide voyaging, massive tsunamis destroyed more than 90% of the Chinese treasure fleet in the Pacific Ocean.

And then, Xuande's plan to disrupt Cahokia-Fengtu to further his self-centered ambitions was far too successful. Unlike in China, where immunity to smallpox outbreaks had grown over the centuries, the heavenly flowers of smallpox inflicted such pandemic annihilation that it led to modern archaeologists naming the middle Mississippi and Ohio valleys "the empty quarter".

And then, in the final chapters of Luo Mao Deng's epic, a council meeting was convened by the chief religious leaders who were part of the command staff of the fleet, and notably did not include Zheng He among those gathered. These leaders disparaged the loss that would be felt back in China by their mass stranding of what would have been largely Mongol cavalry.

> Of course, there will be *some* outcry, but it will surely not last for long before those who may complain will be distracted by something else and forget about these undesirable men entirely.

For these reasons, it is no surprise that both the leaders of Chinese government and its religious leaders would have viewed these events as signs of the depths of heaven's disapproval of the folly and immorality of such overwhelming hubris on the part of Xuande and for his sin against the mandate in advocating intentional destruction of Fengtu. The intentional permanent abandonment of eighteen out of twenty-three of the combination diplomatic, mapping, and military delegations documented by Luo as having been landed on the shores of the Americas, would have only intensified the rage of heaven against Xuande's reign of excess.

Chasing Dragons

So Xuande and his heirs closed China's borders, expelled or confined to limited enclaves every foreigner they could, and outlawed most, if not all, contact with the outside world. They knew that they no longer had a right to the mandate they claimed.

According to the Mandate of Heaven, this "emperor of the entire universe" and his progeny no longer had a true claim to any throne, of any realm, let alone to that of China. The Taoist Master's grand plan destroyed both the dreams of world domination by the civilization which brought the "flowers" and the world of those who received them.

CHAPTER XII

CHINESE CORROBORATION: THE LOACH KING

The identity of the Loach King and the location of his homeland are important evidence for firmly establishing that the Chinese account is centered in America's Mississippi valley. Luo may use the word "loach" here, but China has no fish species that closely fit the description given for the fish being described here by the elder of a Chinese mining colony:

> "...all along the top of its back are points of bone like spear-tips, and it is a rusty red a bit like fresh blood, and far from what you might expect, it moves like the fluttering of a red banner in the wind, moving from place to place in a show and stately manner like an elephant."
>
> The chief Buddhist Missionary asked: "How much damage is it capable of inflicting?"
>
> The colony elder replied: "The loach king only possesses a long tongue, but it can overturn boats that it comes into contact with, accomplishing this with a tail exactly like the harrow it resembles turning over soil in a field, you certainly will not be able to escape from it and get away, not until it has completely finished with sinking your vessel."

In the Americas, there is a fish that fits this description, the lake sturgeon. This fish still grows to incredible size; a 300 pounder was netted in the Missouri River in recent times. Individual sturgeons prior to heavy overfishing in the 19th century could have been much larger, as they could have grown relatively unmolested their entire 150-year life span.

Chasing Dragons

Lake sturgeon

We are not exactly given a specific location for the home territory of the "Loach King" but his lands are those immediately south, down-river, of lands under the direct control of the lord of Fengtu. In Luo's epic, they are described in this way:

> The colony's elder replied: "This individual is a fish king, who holds as his possession as chieftain by right of treaty a region stretching a hundred *lĭ* long, by an average of ten *lĭ* wide …

Referring to him as "a fish king" could make this a reference to that this ruler, aka the Loach King, was some kind of adherent to the worship of, or an earthly avatar of, the Mayan god known as Tlaloc, who was also the god of war. In modern terms, the measurements give for the scope of his dominions a piece of land that is a little over thirty-three miles long by a little over three miles wide, or a little more than 53.6km long and an average of 5.3km wide. Luo goes further, and describes this man's physical appearance:

> …he is soft-spoken and measures to a physical

height more of that of most ordinary men, but his teeth clearly are like those of the men of the kingdom of those who catch birds in nets, but only one of the two has eyes that look to see the honorable light of day. One of these, when occasionally he opens his mouth, the multitudes of the people of the rivers rush to conform to what he commands, their large boats and small travel afar, all doing what is needed that none of them lack for food. And how could any here suffer from a lack of food? When these rivers are high and their flow is violent, their ships reach their destinations swiftly, sailing straight to their goal of reaching his city's gates until they bump directly into them, traveling directly up and into the seat of learning and repository of truth ruled over by this learned and virtuous man...

Luo's account and the historical record tell that the men of Fengtu towered over the Chinese explorers at six-feet or taller on average. This implies that compared to the men of Fengtu, most of the locals along this stretch of the "great river like the Yangtze" were much closer in height to the Chinese explorers. The archaeological record and the historical record both provide an explanation for the cryptic phrase about his teeth – this ruler appears to have undergone tooth modification either by filing or tooth-capping or embedding silver in them, often as the setting for precious stones.

Soon after this, the senior member of the Buddhist delegation on the voyage asks a very interesting question. One whose answer seems to be another wink toward the ancestral lands of those in power overall those living in the Mississippi valley region.

Chasing Dragons

> The chief Buddhist Missionary asked: "Can you tell us this worthy individual's given name?"
> The elder replied: "The given name of this fish king is '*Mājialuō*'."

Luo often transliterated the sounds of the name of the various countries visited by the fleet. Here, he made this ruler's name resemble the name of those who were referred to during the Chinese delegation's earlier visit to Venice—the dangerous "Mai" people. Both of these clearly also resemble the name we refer to their descendants as now—Mayans. This name could be interpreted as giving him the title of the "Dread Lord of the Maya."

The next place spoken of, even further down river, is nearly as easy to identify as Fengtu was as what is now called Cahokia—a very differently arranged mound complex now known as Poverty Point:

> The chief Buddhist Missionary responded: "Many thanks to you, you may be on your way."
> The mining colony elder said: "This minor craftsman still has more problems now that he has to report to his superiors." The chief Buddhist Missionary asked: "And what else has happened that is troubling you?"
> The colony's elder replied: "There is another of these tall mountains built by men in a great port city on the river's edge, this is known as the 'Mountain of the Wind God', and for a very great number of years, this mountain has been the long standing residence of their monkey god and his priesthood, a clever demonic spirit that does great mischief.

The depictions of Poverty Point shown below, all truncate the mound complex one way or another, typically not taking into account what parts of a once much larger complex which archaeologists know was destroyed by flooding and changes in the path of the river bed. The "ghosts" of that larger area the complex once covered can be seen in the aerial photograph and early drawings also give hints that it formerly was formed into full circles. If a full circle, this corroborates the village elder's tale of a city where Ehecatl was worshiped, because his temples and places of worship were always circular in design. Ehecatl, the Meso-American wind god, was one of the forms of Quetzalcoatl, also depicted as a howler monkey wearing a duck-beak mask that covered his mouth. His legends bear a strong resemblance to those of China's Monkey King (*Sun Wukong*), both being tricksters who caused great trouble for the other gods, and both were born from stone.

Aerial view of earthworks at Poverty Point, Louisiana

Old photo showing traces of sections of the Poverty Point mound complex that no longer exist

Location in the state of Louisiana, United States

Luo continues, giving us even more evidence to support that this "Loach King's" lands abutted a realm ruled over by the place that we call Poverty Point.

    Fifty-seven years ago, the god of the West departed for the world beyond and the next individual in line to become their god-emperor was already greatly advanced in age, so his wife was given the rank of co-ruler and the husband and wife served their kingdom as equals on the throne. And what this pair of divine rulers desired was a baby, and as time passed, all of their petitions went unanswered, disrespected by their gods. Therefore one of the priests of the monkey demon and a priestess of their tiger goddess worked together to assist the god emperor, the single-minded efforts of that trio in the river port city had effects that rippled throughout the subjects of that kingdom like a fresh, billowing breeze, drawing a renewal of good fortune and happiness over that city's life like a fog, and this stands directly in the way of our making additional forward progress in both our ship's voyage and the imperial mandate. Our revered Buddhist elder cannot sail unhindered into that port city and move freely about the country it rules, spreading his faith, but, even if we find a way to request to entry, we will need to do so carefully if we desire an opening we can exploit."

Luo has just told us that this mound-builder city in the lower Mississippi River basin had a female co-ruler, just the same as those in later historical records, records that tell us that tribes were sometimes ruled by female chieftains as well as male ones. This is another detail which makes the best candidate to fit the descriptions the Poverty Point Mound Complex in Louisiana.

The rest of the story as told here settles any remaining arguments against this identification. The "American tiger" would later come to be the name of the jaguar in Mandarin. In Mayan lore, the goddess *Ixchel* (Lady Rainbow) was both a jaguar goddess and a patron of motherhood, pregnancy, and childbirth and surprisingly of war too as *Chak Chel* (or goddess O). *Ehecatl* (the monkey/wind god) was also associated with fertility. This would have made them exactly those to whom a childless ruler would have gone in search of a remedy.

Mark Nickless & Laurie Bonner-Nickless

CHAPTER XIII

CHINESE CORROBORATION: LUO'S ACCOUNT OF THE PIASA

Restored original woodcut illustration from Luo's epic

We knew from the start that our claims about the Piasa, even in light of all the rest, are extraordinary—and that extraordinary claims require extraordinary proof. Here is an extraordinary proof of that central claim that started us off in this search for the truth. In Chapter 98 of Luo Mao Deng's *An Account Of The Western World Voyages of the San Bao Eunuch*, is an extraordinary passage describing events which occur on the great river in Feng Tu, on the far side of the world from China:

....And it was still not yet the hour of the goat, when there arose a great tumult of noise. One of the Taoists was enraged that *one side of something had been painted green and the other half red, and that such a surface would provoke the ridicule of heaven, and such inferior work would provoke the ridicule of the locals as well*, and that the flagship must remain there until this was corrected.

The Lord Marshall was in a complete panic, and interceded in the matter, demanding an answer: "What is going on now?"

The Taoist master replied: "That there should be a problem now is exceedingly strange, this was supposed to be *a proper and traditional two-headed rainbow dragon*."

The revered master said: "What is the classical source that was drawn upon for the creation of this two-headed, rainbow dragon?"

The Taoist master answered: "This rainbow dragon is intended to be a depiction of both the yang eastern dragon who appears before the rain comes and the yin western dragon who appears afterwards, their yang and yin natures will join as one to dispel all of these negative energies that have formed to *burn* the faces of the local population."

The revered prince asked: "Since the days of the ancients, the two-headed rainbow dragon has served well as a bringer of peace and harmony, so then what must be done to see to it that it is correctly executed?"

The Taoist master replied: "As is written in the words of the *Yî Yuàn*, it says that in ancient times, there lived a laborer and his only wife. This family which is spoken of lived in the most extreme poverty, and each took a turn at doing without food, because the crops they had raised as their primary source of food had all died, all before they could fully mature and ripen in the sun, finally they decided that they were in such a state of ruin that they would have to sell their prized fighting bull, for this reason, forever afterwards, that time of terrible personal sacrifice and extreme disharmony. An auspicious omen. Also there has been handed down to us, though from a non-Taoist source, a poem and song which might prove my point if I might recite it now? As that poem says:

> Have you been revived once more by that sweet unspoken poetry in the air?
> I turn again to look back to that star-lit isle,
> To refined charms that stand the test of time on those distant banks.
> Since I am a soldier I am called upon to stay strong,
> Yet again, I must return with my comrades to scenes of profound disharmony.
> In moments of leisure, great beauty can be cherished,
> The fortunate spirit expends itself in the writing of golden words of poetry.
> If only you could hold me back longer from taking up again my blood-stained blade,
> In the end as always before, I will fail to serve the desires of my heart."

The Lord Admiral San Bao spoke then, saying: "The yin and yang dragon is clearly what should be the proper goal for we want to display here, which makes it even more appropriate that we would expect that the most capable Taoist master would want to be so kind as to volunteer to take charge of correcting any errors in it."

Appropriately, the Taoist master protested: "When so asked I do not dare to be so bold as to refuse and shirk my duty!"

Chasing Dragons

But even as he said this that clever man was already seeking ways in which he might twist this situation to his advantage, by any one of a dozen of the tricks of his trade that he knew so that his return to China would not be interfered with. The Taoist master's tactic was not to stand idle and wait, but to be ceaselessly prodding and pressing his suit like an industrious swarm of bees. Day after day, wearing down the spirits of those who challenged him, until he was rid of their opposition.

Suddenly, there rang out another loud and echoing cry, it was about the two rainbow dragons, and in reference the morning's work that was not entirely finished on the long, thin, pair of yin and yang rainbow dragons. As luck would have it, the work would have to be stopped for the day because the weather was once again deteriorated into heavy fog. You could not see the palm of your hand if you extended your arm out in front of you. You could not even see a person standing beside you.

The revered senior master asked: "Again a heavy fog has rolled in, why do these conditions keep arising?"

The Taoist master replied: "This fog is an obstacle to stop the progress of our work, and this ship is acting as an anchor point to hold it to surface of the waters, but there is no reason that we should continue to suffer these conditions."

The revered prince asked: "So why does this adversity keep coming upon us? We have made every effort to seek be on good terms with the Yellow Emperor, and are ignorant of any outstanding wrongdoing that could bring this kind of resistance against us, yet this is a supernatural battle which we cannot win. The Yellow Emperor rules far away on Mount Tai, and for three days and three nights, we have suffered this profoundly fog-bound weather. There are a number of women who serve him, with human heads, and the delicate bodies of birds. And the yellow Emperor has them inform him of all wrong-doing, investigating it before returning once more to bow low before their master, kowtowing and not daring to arise. These maidens, who serve him, speak to him, saying:

> 'We are your marvelous heavenly daughters
> and this is the truth. What do you wish done
> in this place? What do you wish to not see
> written?'

And the yellow emperor (*Wù shì shān zhōng zǐ*)...would reply, saying:

> 'These young men desired to fight ten
> thousand wars of conquest, and have hidden
> ten thousand secrets from view, by what
> method should we encourage them to leave
> this place?'

The celestial maidens would answer him, saying:

> 'Use plentiful fog to attack them, give them
> ten thousand defeats, a normal seeming fog
> but all concealing, as they hid their ten
> thousand from view in all ways cover them.'

Couldn't this be what is to now blame for the conditions that we are suffering under? As Liang Futing wrote for our edification in his carefully constructed 'Morning Mist Poem':

> River fog mingles with mountain mists,
> So deep, it drives the dawn from the sky.
> Heed the gentle manner of the gibbon
> who sits and ponders on the mountain,
> then be aware of the reputation of the otter
> who dwells in the river.
> The bewildered fisherman stands on the

river bank unsure of what to do,
Perplexed over how best to guide his boat
along the river's edge.
The mists rise into the air at each day's end,
Settling down to delicately
cloak all waters."

The Lord Admiral San Bao spoke again then, asking: "That the two rainbow dragons cannot be worked on when the weather is excessively foggy, is more than a little strangely appropriate, but then, when will conditions be good enough that our artisans will be able to complete them?"

The Taoist master replied: "This poor Taoist can mend all this and get the men back to work on the bluff face just as before." This was easy for the Taoist master to say, and to say with certainty, "just as before," because long before this work stoppage occurred he had already worked out how he might handle such a situation if their official departure was delayed.

A sound pierced through the heavy fog just then, a sudden and violent, massive and discordant splash. It came down on the bow of the ship, and as luck would have it, it was a very old dead pine tree that had fallen there, one the appeared to be so old that it's trunk neither bore any branches, nor had any roots at its base, and was no longer strong or growing, and despite the loudness of the splash was not a large tree, and now it rested impaled in the deck of the bow of the flagship as it had once stood, in a straight vertical position exactly like a calligrapher's brush.

The revered elder master exclaimed: "Now, yet another unexpected turn of events has occurred, a little old pine tree, people going to get upset about this as well!"

The revered senior prince responded: "Your men

would regard this pine tree as a very important thing, how then can we combat many of them becoming worried about this?"

The Taoist master asked in return: "Gossip by our men about this one pine tree is going to immediately cause us difficulties?

The revered senior prince responded: "In that case, my friend, how do we stop this from becoming a costly situation?"

The Taoist master replied: "Whenever some of the savages from the mountain country come up this part of the river, these new *curly-bearded guardian dragons* will look down upon them as our envoys, their coloring might not be what is customary, but we are being dragged along by one hundred other curses right now that urgently seek to compel our departure. The savages who see these will ask each other, saying:

'What monarch governs this place? And, how
fast can we get out of here?'

And such a pair of envoys as these will answer on our behalf, saying:
'The men of a great company came to this
place and stopped here to affix this on the
face of the bluff. And afterwards those
faithful men longed for home and family, and
they did not wish linger any longer in this
foreign land, therefore they departed with all
possible speed when this was done.'

This will make the savages' hair stand on end, and our 'envoys' will have far more of an impact than any ancient pine tree that fell down and impaled itself in our deck.

Ignorant men may worship ancient pine trees and

treat them with respect, but surely they will bow down in even greater admiration before the likes of what we have affixed to this hillside, and it will drive off those ignorant savages in white-faced terror from the curse we left on this place. Overlooking how this tough old grandfather might have been properly dealt with in the past, these savages might question the source of this misfortune. The ancient grandfather of all pine trees itself might speak to them, saying:

> 'From now on, shouldn't you conform to what these new bearded dragons tell you to do? It is plain that their regulation is to relieve the uneasiness of your minds.'

The savages' elders will recognize this, and know from whence these envoys came to them for their benefit because of the seedling of the old pine tree we planted in its place. When that pine tree is fully matured from a seedling, won't that solve this matter of honor?"

The revered senior prince replied: "The Ming Emperor of China will want to pay compensation to the people of the mountain for this unfortunate and unexpected turn of events, then the sound of the bells on our horses' harnesses will be seen as fortunate in the western territories, and the current troubles can be known to finally be over! It is taboo in China to leave a withered pine tree to fall without replacing it with a live seedling, with dark blue-green branches and foliage, freshly planted as a replacement in the same spot as its predecessor. Forgetting this will bring the consequence of calamity later and destroy the internal peace and tranquility of families, but the sweet blessings of prosperity return when it is observed, so I submit that this withered pine tree might actually be considered a good omen, now isn't that not too costly a solution to this matter?"

The Taoist master replied: "This natural stage has a rather loose and crumbling surface, and while this allows for a natural entrance into the burial cave at the base of the cliff face, it still forces the disc above it to be pressed in close to the natural outcropping like a grain storage tower on one side, and the main part of the entrance at its fullest width is conspicuously narrow, at only four to five chi wide. Though height of this rampart is properly impressive, the width of the opening nevertheless makes one flinch at so grievously narrow and cramped a state of affairs, and I am concerned that we are not simply availing ourselves of the easier route of just sticking a branch in place, a branch with abundant foliage, this has elements which are both on a proper imperial scale and cramped, vigorous and crippled, grandeur and scholarship are bound up and superseded in such conditions, how can all that be counted as a noble and correct thing?"

The revered senior prince replied: "The tall pillars like grain silos elicit quiet sighs of acclaim like peaks of mountains, speaking to us as if to say:

> 'Together, we stand like lords of the forest measuring as straight and tall as any pine tree, although the rock that forms us is made of a massive number of strata, we are imposing enough to be used to build great edifices, when you desire to build great mansions this is what men use'.

Doesn't that seem more what strangers who see this in future would say? As Lǐ Délín said in his carefully crafted verses:
> Sturdy roots grow in the Imperial gardens,
> Rising up into graceful branches beside a

splendid reflecting pool.
Regardless of the cold season of the year,
their beauty does not fail,
At New Year's it is a lovely as the time of
falling leaves.
The leaves swirl down
like a rain of golden dew,
When the languid breezes blow
through the eucalyptus trees.
Give exceedingly great thanks
to the frost and snow,
Since it is truly certain that without them
the leaves would never fall.

The Lord Admiral San Bao spoke then, saying: "As always, my two most senior commanders cannot while away the hours without troubling the rest of us with these pointless debates. If only for this one day, settle this divisiveness between you, *the paint for our intertwined rainbow dragons may not adhere well today because of this heavy fog*; but it is only one day of heavy fog, and you must restrain yourselves from acting rashly just because of one very old pine tree, and this construction project in this place of bewitching wonders and wicked cleverness has a definite time limit, so for this moment set aside all this infighting. Rise above it henceforth and replace animosity with cooperation in the hours ahead, otherwise how can we possibly guide this fleet to complete its long journey? Otherwise, how will we be able to make our final report to our emperor, may he live ten thousand years, that we have fulfilled his mandate?"

Mark Nickless & Laurie Bonner-Nickless

CHAPTER XIV

A MYSTERY ON THE PERIPHERY: THE FINAL PROOF

The Piasa Bone Cave

One of the more outlandish aspects of Russell's Piasa mythology was his lurid description of the "Piasa bone cave," located near the Piasa painting. There, the great *winged* monster devoured its victims and left their remains to accumulate in the floor of its cavernous nest. Russell claimed to have visited this cave, and his vivid description survives in the 1887 *Records of Ancient Races in the Mississippi Valley*, compiled by William McAdams. It is a classic example of Russell's Victorian predilection for hyperbole:

> Preceded by an intelligent guide, who carried a spade, I set out on my excursion. The cave was extremely difficult of access, and at one point in our progress I stood at an elevation of one hundred and fifty feet on the perpendicular face of the bluff, with barely room to sustain one foot. The unbroken wall towered above me, while below was the river. After a long and perilous climb, we reached the cave, which was about fifty feet above the surface of the river. By the aid of a long pole placed on a projecting rock, and the upper end touching the mouth of the cave, we succeed in entering it. Nothing could be more impressive than the view from the entrance to the cavern. The Mississippi was rolling in silent grandeur beneath us. High over our heads a single cedar tree hung its branches over the cliff, and on one of the dead dry limbs was seated a bald eagle. No other sign of life was near us, a Sabbath stillness rested on the scene. Not a cloud was visible on the heavens; not a

Chasing Dragons

breath of air was stirring. The broad Mississippi was before us, calm and smooth as a lake. The landscape presented the same wild aspect it did before it had met the eye of the white man.

The roof of the cavern was vaulted, and the top was hardly less than, twenty feet high. The shape of the cavern was irregular; but so far as I could judge the bottom would average twenty by thirty feet. The floor of the cavern throughout its whole extent was one mass of human bones. Skulls and other bones were mingled in the utmost confusion. To what depth they extended I was unable to decide; but we dug to the depth of 3 or 4 feet in every part of the cavern, and still we found only bones. The remains of thousands must have been deposited here. How and by whom, and for what purpose, it is impossible to conjecture.

Unlikely as it seems, there is a historic basis for a Piasa bone cave. Ironically, it is also recorded by McAdams, a few more pages along, and serves as a factual counterpoint.

In reciting the tradition of the Piasa, in the first chapter of this volume, Mr. Russell makes mention of a cavern in the bluff below the mouth of the Illinois River, and referred to as one of the fastnesses to which the monster took his victims to be devoured at leisure. In his visit to this cavern he describes it as containing a great quantity of human bones.

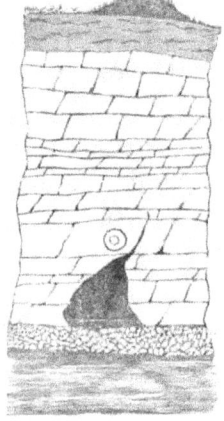

There is a cavern just below the town of Grafton, known for many years as the "Bone Cave." The outer part of the cavern was simply a huge crevice, open at both ends and extending for some little distance parallel with the river. This part of the cave was twenty to thirty feet in width and perhaps a hundred feet long. The sides of the crevice came together above and formed a roof fifteen or twenty feet in height. The cave, being perfectly sheltered from rain and storms, was very dry; and the floor was covered to the depth of several feet with dust and various debris, consisting of pieces of stone, bones of animals, ashes, charred sticks, pieces of pottery, with some human remains. In the days of the early white settlers, this cavernous place, which was partially lighted from each open end, was the resort, in inclement or cold weather, for the domestic animals of the neighborhood.

At the lower end of the great cave-shelter we have described, at Grafton, was the entrance to a lateral opening that went at right angles directly into the bluff. This is connected with the illustration of the entrance, showing the bone-cave. We give a situation of the mouth, with one of the circular hieroglyphs, or pictographs, on a ledge of rock above the opening. On the top of the bluff is seen one of the ancient mounds so common in this region. Below the entrance to the cave is shown some of the debris of loose rocks; and still further down, the shore of the Mississippi, which in very high water approaches near but has never been known to rise so high, by several feet, as to enter the cavern. The triangular- shaped opening to this part of the cavern gave a somewhat difficult access to an inner chamber, not so large as the outer part we have described.

The floor of this second chamber is also covered with dust, and an accumulation of bones, pottery, ornaments and stone implements, like the outer cave. The first white settlers say that in their early occupation of the region many human bones could be seen in the inner cavern. In our excavations we found a great number of bones, some of which had been those of human beings. Most of these, like the bones of the animals, had been broken; giving one an impression of cannibalism. Some of the human bones, however, were whole, and we obtained one nearly perfect skull...

The scene described by this passage is a far cry from Russell's ghastly cavern piled several feet deep with human bones. McAdams' cave entrance was at ground level and easily accessible. Early white settlers did find a few bones in it, which they identified as human and animal. A single human skull was found. It is clear from the description of debris that both Whites and Indians had sheltered in the cave for a long time. No self-respecting monster would have dwelt in such a vulnerable and lowly place! The accompanying sketch confirms the seemingly ordinary nature of the bone cave—except in one aspect. Above the cave is an unusual "circular hieroglyph," carved in stone. McAdams continues: "The mound shown in the engraving as being immediately over the cavern has been excavated away, with, a part of the bluff, in the operations of a stone-quarry; and that part of the cliff which a few years ago was adorned with the great red hieroglyphic eye, and the cavern's mouth below, was taken away to build the Lindell and Southern hotels, those prided caravansaries of the City of St. Louis. It is said that the very stone that has this Indian manitou, as the early Jesuits called it, was built into the walls of the Lindell."

Construction of the Lindell Hotel began in 1857, was interrupted by legal problems, and resumed in 1859. The quarrying of the Piasa site to build the village of Elsah began in 1854. It accelerated in 1857, when Semple reorganized his holdings in order to earn a profit. The chronology fits perfectly. The limestone used for building the Lindell hotel and the village of Elsah are almost certainly from the same source—Semple's quarry. If the Piasa was indeed constructed by the Chinese, as we have posited, then the nearby Piasa Bone Cave, complete with a circle carved above it, should appear in Luo's *An Account of The Western World Travels of the San Bao Eunuch*.

Indeed, it does in chapter 98.

The passage concerns the burial cave of Lu. He was an artisan who oversaw the construction of the adjacent "yin-yang rainbow dragons" — the Piasa. Tragically, Lu died before the completion of the monument that defined the western limit of Ming world exploration. Even the circle is mentioned: The Daoist master replied: "This natural stage has a rather loose and crumbling surface, and while this allows for a natural entrance into the burial cave at the base of the cliff face, it still forces the disc above it to be pressed in close to the natural outcropping like a grain storage tower on one side, and the main part of the entrance at its fullest width is conspicuously narrow, four to five *chi* wide." [31]

So here we have parallel descriptions, in English and Chinese, of two burials in small caves. Both caves had carved circles above their entrances. Both lay near arches occupied by two dragons, along great rivers near great cities, at a point far distant from the civilized Old World.

Both caves were located at the base of great cliffs, near the level of great rivers, which is surprising, as those caves would surely flood. Who would pick a final resting place for a revered comrade where flood would disturb his peace, unless they were unfamiliar with the great rivers' ways? It could not have been an Indian burial, for they knew the river's ebb and flow. Besides, McAdams states that the Indian graves he saw were in a line atop the cliff.

Why was the grave marked with a red circle? To the Chinese, the color red is a powerful symbol. Mirroring the lamb's blood at the Jewish Passover, red painted over a door was protection against pernicious spirits. The red circle above the Piasa bone cave entrance lasted for centuries. The Indians used several red pigments, such as iron oxide or ochre. These pigments have survived, in a few cases, on fired pots found in caves, and some red-tinted petroglyphs have been found in rock shelters, protected from the elements. But these colors have not survived on petroglyphs that were carved in open, exposed places. China Red, made from sulfur and cinnabar, was the most enduring red pigment of antiquity. Its use would explain the

---

31 Three *chi* are equal to approximately one meter, so this was about one & one-third to one & two- thirds meters in width.

unusual longevity of the red circle.

Could the circular hieroglyph/disc have been a pearl?

Another powerful Chinese symbol, a pearl, can symbolize *genius in obscurity*. There is more. Not only does Luo's account mirror the McAdams description, it agrees with a detail in Lewis' original painting, which previously seemed to have no significance. There is a singular tree atop the bluff that appears to be a conifer of some sort. It is gnarled and twisted as is so typical of specimens living atop the exposed river-bluffs. To the Chinese, the cedar, and especially the pine, both evergreens, represent steadfastness, longevity and old age.

Incredibly, again in chapter 98, Luo describes an incident during which an ancient pine tree fell from atop the bluff and impaled itself in the bow of a Chinese boat that was moored tight against the bank, near the yin-yang dragon arch construction site. In its place, a pine seedling was planted, in the expectation that a mature tree would remind the "savages," for generations to come, that Zheng He's envoys came for their benefit. (An ironic attitude, indeed, after introducing a plague!) The Chinese planted the pine, and Henry Lewis saw it as a mature, gnarled specimen some four hundred years later.

Now we have a clearer understanding of the Piasa Bone Cave's true story, based on parallel accounts written centuries apart. Master Lu was buried in a cave adjacent to the dragon arch—the Piasa—which he had helped create. There was a red circle, perhaps a pearl, carved above its entrance. It testified to the importance of the man entombed within as it stood guard for centuries over his lonely grave, sadly abandoned in a strange land so far from home. Above this bittersweet place, atop a lofty cliff, a memorial pine grew to maturity and was immortalized in Lewis' painting. These three accounts, two recorded in ink and one in paint, clearly describe the same burial site— in America.

So, as reconstructed by Laurie, here are the Piasa dragons:

Here is the Piasa, as painted by Henry Lewis. Here are the gnarled pine above, the Piasa bone cave below, and the enigmatic circle above its opening.

But this extraordinary story is not yet complete.

Chao Chen—an honest-to-goodness rocket scientist—was our fellow presenter in Malacca, Malaysia, in 2010. While we do not always agree with him on some details, we must agree that he has brought to light a crucial fact. The Chinese mythological creature that guarded tombs is called a "Pi Xui."

The Chinese "x" is pronounced much like our "s."

Thus, Pi Xui … Piasa….

Could this be a mere coincidence?

Chasing Dragons

CHAPTER XV

A SUMMARY OF THE WORK – ANSWERS

In this book we have made known our discoveries of the answers to several historical mysteries, documenting our conclusions step-by-step. Following is a summary of the mysteries, all of which are inter-related, as we will show.

Mystery #1: What is the origin and meaning of the enigmatic *Piasa* monsters painting discovered by the explorer Marquette on a river bluff at Elsah, Illinois? And why did the *Piasa* vanish for decades, then reappear in another version in nearby Alton?
Answer #1: The original Piasa was a painting of two Chinese dragons, the *lōng,* an Imperial symbol, in commemoration of the visit of the fleet of Admiral Zheng He around the year 1433. The painting of today is a misinterpretation of the original painting and is located in a different place. The original bluff upon which the painting was made was quarried away in the late 1850s.

Mystery #2: Why did the population of the Mississippi Valley suffer a decimation in the mid-1400s?
Answer #2: A scheme by a Taoist priest to introduce a minor epidemic of smallpox to Cahokia to destabilize the Mississippian culture went terribly awry. Because the inhabitants had *no* resistance to smallpox—unlike the people of China—a devastating pandemic killed the majority of people in the Middle Mississippi *and* Ohio Valleys in the years following 1433.

Mystery #3: Is there any other evidence, as claimed by Menzies and others, that the fleet of Chinese Admiral *Zheng He* visited North America in the 1400s?

Answer #3: The Piasa painting itself is one proof. The 16th century author Luo Mao Deng's *An Account of the Western World Voyages of the San Bao Eunuch* is a second proof. His book's last chapters describe Admiral Zheng He's last voyage to a destination which is clearly in North America. Luo includes a detailed account of the Piasa's creation and vividly describes interactions and confrontations with people who have a distinctively Mississippian culture.

Mystery #4: Why was the immense Chinese fleet burned and Chinese world exploration ended after the return of the seventh *Zheng He* global expedition?

Answer #4: The disaster at Cahokia and the subsequent abandonment of North America led to the loss of "The Mandate of Heaven", which constituted the sole authority of the Ming Dynasty to be rulers of China, so all exploration ceased, the fleet was burned, and most records destroyed.

Chasing Dragons

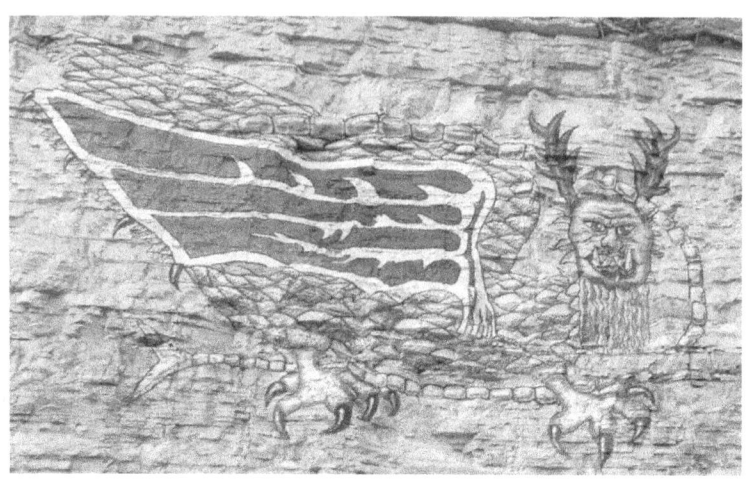

The Piasa now, Alton, Illinois –
*A poorly-done misrepresentation of the original
Photo by Lauri Nickless, 2018*

The Original Piasa – 1432.
Recreated by Laurie Nickless, 2018

Even as this new edition was being formatted for publication, we made an important discovery.

There is another Piasa image, which was drawn by writer-illustrator John Caspar Wild. Because Wild died in 1846, it is likely that his sketch slightly predates the Henry Lewis painting of the Piasa.

Both depictions closely agree on the general appearance of the Piasa, but there are some important differences in the details.

The Wild version shows flames fully surrounding the central Precious Pearl. These flames are identical to those surrounding the Precious Pearl on the Nanjing memorial. The crude smile seen on Lewis' Pearl is not present, proof that the vandals had been busy between the two artists.

On the lower left of Wild's Piasa, the outline of a head can be seen. It is larger than Lewis' devil head and has a long fox-like snout, just as does a Chinese dragon.

Chasing Dragons

It is difficult for us to parse out more detail from Wild's Piasa for a simple reason. Someone in the distant past erased the outline of the Piasa, but not the landscape of trees and bluffs outside it.

What we see today are white streaks where Wild had originally sketched strong clear lines. Presently, as of May 2019, a friend of ours is preparing to visit the Library of Congress and find a copy of Wild's original work. Hopefully it will prove unredacted.

Henry Lewis' lithograph, "Der Piasa Felsen"
from Das Illustrirte Mississipithal, published in 1857.

All that remains today of the original limestone bluff where the Piasa was painted, after extensive quarrying in the late 1850s

CHAPTER XVI

PIASA TIMELINE AND REFERENCES

Here we summarize and document the significant events and dates discussed in detail in relevant earlier chapters. Subsequent to submitting this manuscript, other sources have confirmed that Admiral Zhang He's fleet did visit and map the Americas. It is our hope that this book will stimulate further research in support of these remarkable discoveries.

2200 BC – Record of possible visit of Chinese explorers to the Americas during Xia dynasty compiled by the great Yu at the request of Emperor Shun, who would later abdicate in favor of Yu.
Source:
1. Charlotte Harris Rees. *SECRET MAPS OF THE ANCIENT WORLD*. Author House, 1663 Liberty Drive, Bloomington, IN. 2008.

1200 BC-Shang Chinese flee to America. There they settle and become Olmec culture.
Source:
1. www.jstor.org/stable/24536189?seq=1#page_scan_tab_contents

502 AD—Buddhist monk, Hui Shen, returns to China after an absence of many years. He reports to the Emperor Wu Ti that he and his party have explored a vast land on the eastern rim of the Pacific Ocean-- the fabled land of Fu Sang. Hui's report was duly filed away and nearly lost in the vaults of the Imperial bureaucracy.
Source:
1. Charlotte Harris Rees. *SECRET MAPS OF THE ANCIENT WORLD*. Author House, 1663 Liberty Drive, Bloomington, IN. 2008.

865 AD – By their own report, the people of Fengtu-Cahokia come

north, following the migrating hummingbirds, leaving *Feng Du La* (now Guatemala) to settle in the Mississippi Valley, leaving their ancestral lands to escape a time of severe political and social unrest.
Source:
1. Luo Mao Deng. *THE WESTERN WORLD VOYAGES OF THE SAN BAO EUNUCH.* China, 1585.

Early MING DYNASTY (1368-1644) before 1405—A Chinese ship loses its masts in a typhoon and drifts to the Pacific Coast of North America. Fu Sang is rediscovered. After the masts are replaced using massive trees the crew finds there, the ship returns home and they report their discovery.
Source:
1. Ibid.

1405 through 1421—The shipyards of Nanjing churn out a vast fleet of technically advanced ships for a golden age of world exploration under Admiral Zheng He. The Ming Treasure Fleet visits America and begins a survey of the rediscovered land. Maps are known to have been drawn in 1408 and 1418. Liu Gang, a fellow presenter at the Royal Geographical Society London, April 15, 2012, discovered a copy of the 1418 map in a Shanghai antique shop and purchased it, in 2001, for the equivalent of $500.
Sources:
1. Menzies, Gavin. *1421 THE YEAR CHINA DISCOVERED AMERICA.* Harper Collins Publishers Inc. 10 East 53rd Street, New York, NY 10022. 2002.
2. Personal contact.

1421, at the latest—Jin Bifeng, respected Buddhist elder and Confucian scholar visits Feng Tu, known today as Cahokia.
Source:
1. Luo Mao Deng. *THE WESTERN WORLD VOYAGES OF THE SAN BAO EUNUCH* China, 1585.
1432—The Chinese plan to revisit their known world to announce

the ascension of the Emperor Xuande, and to bring Buddhism to the barbarians who live in the great city of Feng Tu. They also plan to exploit their previous discovery of massive iron deposits found in the low mountains south of that city.
Source:
1. Ibid.

1433—Cahokia is revisited, with disastrous results. A smallpox epidemic wipes out the very people who were to be converted to Buddhism. Before leaving, the Piasa is constructed. Lu, the unfortunate Chinese engineer in charge of the project dies, and is buried in a nearby cave. A skull is unearthed in his burial cave by early 19th- century American settlers.
Sources:
1. Ibid.
2. *THE PIASA or THE DEVIL AMONG THE INDIANS*. E.B. Fletcher, Book and Job Printer. Morris ILL. 1887.

1434—Upon their return home in Nanjing, Chinese sailors erect a memorial to their voyage. The stone memorial is capped by two dragons carved within an arch. It matches both Marquette's written description and Lewis' painting, down to trivial details. The Chinese then burn their capital ships and most of the official records of their voyages. Never again will China dominate the seas.
Sources:
1. Personal observation in Nanjing.
2. Voelker, Frederick E. "The Piasa." *Journal of the Illinois State Historical Society* (1908-1984), vol. 7, no. 1, 1914, pp. 82–91. JSTOR./
3. Lewis, Henry. "Der Piasa Felsen," *DAS ILLUSTRIERTE MISSISSIPPITHAL*, Dusseldorf: Arnz & Company. 1854.

13th-15th Centuries, Mongol or Ming Dynasty-Asian horses introduced to American West. Exact dates unknown.
Source:

https://www.horsetalk.co.nz/2018/08/02/genetic-links-siberian-asian-horses-north-dakota/

Illustration from Chapter 23 of Luo's epic *"An Account of the Western World Voyages of the San Bao Eunuch"*. Note similarities to Appaloosa breed found in the Northwest plains of North America.

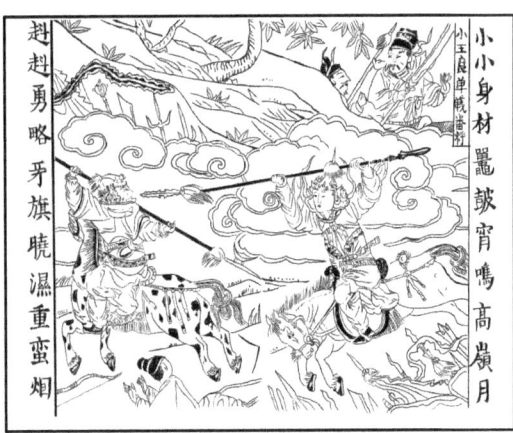

1602 – Using Chinese sources, Mateo Ricci draws a world map showing "Feng Du La" in Mayan territory in what would become Central America. This supports claims made by the people of Fengtu beginning in Chapter 87 of Luo's epic that their ancestral lands lay very far to the south.

Sources:
1. Kunyu Wanguo Quantu , 坤輿萬國全圖, or 1602 Ricci Map.
2. Luo Mao Deng. *THE WESTERN WORLD VOYAGES OF THE SAN BAO EUNUCH*, China, 1585.

Central America as shown in 1602 Ricci Map, showing

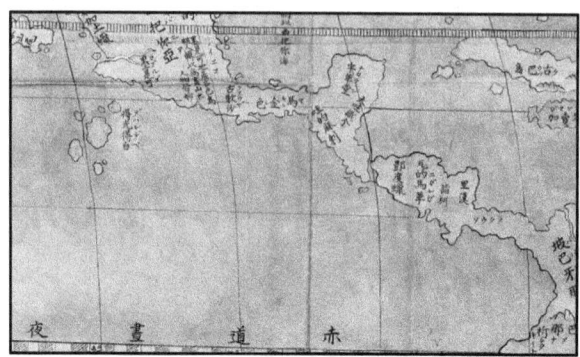 

"Feng Tu La" (酆度蠟 -- Country where the rituals associated with the New Year are strictly practiced) The words "Feng Du La" are shown magnified)

1673—While exploring the Mississippi River, Father Marquette stumbles upon the painted Piasa bas-relief and pens his famous description. Soon, local inhabitants acquire guns and proceed to shoot up the feared Piasa.
Source:
1. Voelker, Frederick E. "The Piasa." *Journal of the Illinois State Historical Society* (1908-1984), vol. 7, no. 1, 1914, pp. 82–91. JSTOR.

1682 – LaSalle reports *something* Chinese on the Ohio River.
Source:
1. Nicolas de La Salle, THE LA SALLE EXPEDITION ON THE MISSISSIPPI RIVER, 1682. Edited by William C. Foster. Translated by Johanna L. Warren: Texas State Historical Association, 2003.

1753—Bauche's official French map of North America is published. The west coast of Canada is clearly labeled as Fu Sang of the Chinese.
Source:
1. *Considérations géographiques et physiques sur les découvertes nouvelles dans la grande mer* (Paris, 1754).

1836—Professor John Russell begins penning a series of imaginative tales for publication in *FAMILY MAGAZINE* which transform the two monsters of the Piasa into a solitary giant man-eating bird. This rewriting of history makes him famous and wealthier.
Source:
1. //www.illinoishistory.com/piasabird.html

1846 or slightly earlier-Swiss born artist and writer John Caspar Wild sketches his version of the Piasa for the serialized publication, THE VALLEY OF THE MISSISSIPPI ILLUSTRATED.

1846—Henry Lewis paints DER PIASA FELSEN, a faithful rendering of the Piasa, for his German language travelogue Das Illustrirte Mississippithal.
Source:
1. Lewis, Henry. "Der Pias Felen," *DAS ILLUSTRIERTE MISSISSIPPITHAL*, (Dusseldorf: Arnz & Company, 1854.)

Circa **1853**—A leading proponent of Manifest Destiny, Senator James Semple, recognizes the problematic nature of the Piasa. (Our conclusion).

1856- Semple buys the property on which it is located and then systematically destroys the painting, using the limestone rubble to construct the village of Elsah. The Piasa is gone by 1856. (The date is our conclusion).

Source:
1. Hosmer, Charles B. Jr. and Williams, Paul O. *ELSAH; A HISTORICAL GUIDEBOOK,* Fifth Edition, Revised. Elsah, Illinois: Historic Elsah Foundation, 1986.

1880s—Banker and amateur archaeologist George H. Dougherty concludes the Piasa was Chinese.
Source:
1. jersey.illinoisgenweb.org/newspaper/clippings2.htm

1891—A new version of the Piasa is copyrighted and is soon used on bottles of Pitt's Black Liniment and other products. It is this unauthentic Piasa that has come down to the present.
Source:
1. Maruna, Scott. *THE CURIOUS PERSON'S GUIDE TO THE HISTORY AND MYSTERY OF THE PIASA BIRD.* Jacksonville, Illinois: Swamp Gas Book Company. 2005.

1924—E. W. Payne, another banker and archaeologist, writes "a superficial examination of the painting shows that it is undoubtedly a Chinese Dragon."
Source:
1. www.newspapers.com/newspage/140263851/

1925—A Piasa "Bird", based on the horrific 1891 version, is painted on a bluff in Alton, many miles south of its original location.
Source:
1. Ibid.

2004—Researcher Mark Nickless, unaware of Dougherty and Payne, independently conducts his own investigation, concluding that the Piasa was painted by a Chinese party commanded by Admiral Zheng He sometime around 1421. A short article he writes on this appears in the October/November 2004 edition of the *OUTDOOR GUIDE MAGAZINE.*

2005—Mark Nickless is invited to Nanjing, China to present a paper on his Piasa research, at the International Academic Forum in Memory of the 600th Anniversary of the Sailing of Zheng He's Fleet. He speaks on July 5th. While flying home, an excited Chinese-American tells him that the city of Nanjing has been "turned upside down" by the excitement generated by an American proving China had visited America in 1421.

2006—Following a cryptic lead she finds in Louise Levathes' *When China Ruled The Seas*, Laurie Nickless, ably assisted by St. Louis businessman Jim Kennedy and retired Chinese Admiral Zheng Ming, acquires a copy of the second half of an obscure book written in 1585 by Luo Mao Deng. It is *An Account of the Western World Voyages of the San Bao Eunuch*. Laurie begins its translation from archaic literary Mandarin. She is cautioned by Hong Kong businessman and movie producer, Frank Lee, that no one understands the book and that attempts to do so would "lead to madness". Nevertheless, she perseveres. Luo's book proves to be a highly detailed account of a visit to America in 1433. The completion of the Piasa is described in Chapter 98.

2010—Laurie and Mark Nickless invited to Malacca, Malaysia. On July 7, they spoke about Feng Tu and the Piasa at the International Conference Zheng He and the Afro-Asian World.

2012—Laurie and Mark Nickless spoke at the Royal Geographical Society, London. They had been invited by RGS member, Gavin Menzies, author of *1421, The Year China Discovered America*. Menzies' ground-breaking book has sold many millions of copies in over 135 countries, in many languages. Laurie's reconstruction of the Piasa appeared on Phoenix TV News, Hong Kong.

2012—Publication of first version of *Chasing Dragons,* (privately printed edition)

2017—Publication of first edition of *TO THE GATES OF FENGTU*.

2019—The International Cartographic Association publishes an important paper by Dr. Siu-Leung Lee,
China Mapped America before 1430.
Source:
http://www.readcube.com/articles/10.5194%2Fica-proc-1-67-2018?fbclid=IwAR38tQFDnvNgQy2HxdFwrCN_F3euvYahfJ-48QqeD7iSzGBKUq18Soke6So

2019 - Mark and Laurie Nickless present a slide show of their work at Plenary Session 1 of the Fifth Zheng He International Peace Forum at Surabaya, Indonesia. Their presentation is judged Best Paper of the Forum, and they win a cash prize.

2019—Publication of the expanded and definitive edition of *Chasing Dragons,* by Talisman House Press, an imprint of Hydra Publications, LLC., Goshen, Kentucky

Mark Nickless & Laurie Bonner-Nickless

ABOUT THE AUTHORS

In 2004, Mark Nickless and his wife, Laurie Bonner-Nickless, started work on what would later come to be known as the "Piasa Project," with an article called "Was the Piasa, in Fact, a Chinese Dragon?" published in Outdoor Guide Magazine. Since then, they have presented papers & lectures at international conferences in Nanjing, China (2005), and Melaka, Malaysia(2010), and were invited guest lecturers at a gathering at the Royal Geographical Society in London (2012). Mr. Nickless received a B.A. in Education, in 1976, from Missouri Baptist University, St. Louis, Missouri. He has worked for more than twenty years teaching in special education. Mr. Nickless is a Mensan who is a current member of Missouri Outdoor Communicators. He is happiest when paddling his kayak in pursuit of chain pickerel or wet-wading an Ozark trout stream. Ms. Bonner-Nickless received an A. S. in Cinematography, from Moorpark College, in Moorpark, California, in 1983, and a B. S. in Telecommunications from Southwest Baptist University, in Bolivar, Missouri, in 1990. Both degrees were pursued with a heavy emphasis on writing for those mediums. Ms. Bonner-Nickless is a past member of Missouri Outdoor Communicators (both as an outdoor journalist and a web master.) She has won awards for her poetry, and artwork, and wrote a column on harvesting and cooking wild edibles for several years. They live near De Soto, Missouri, with their two daughters—Ekaterina, age 22 (now a graduate of Truman University), and Samantha, age 18, who are both budding writers and artists. The Nickless' also share their home with an opinionated & well-fed cat named Fawkes, who like all of her kind firmly believes that she's perpetually starving, and that what the world truly needs is her as it's (mostly) benevolent despot. Fawkes absolutely adores humans (especially when served raw with a hearty dollop of gravy and a dash of salt).

Chasing Dragons

A PERSONAL CONNECTION

The easternmost outpost of the Mississippian Culture was the city of Xaora, in the Catawba Valley of North Carolina. Xaora was founded late compared to Cahokia, sometime in the 1400s. Based on early French maps, at least one researcher concluded that Xaora was founded by Cahokians of noble class who had mysteriously moved east and resettled, becoming the Catawba tribe.

I have an illustrious ancestor, George Heinrich Witmar. Nineteenth century family lore says he was the illegitimate son of a notorious nobleman in the German state of Sax-Coburg. Heinrich had no prospects there, and so he came to America. Here, he anglicized his name to Henry Whitener. His son, also Henry, was the first white settler in the Catawba Valley.

During the American Revolution, this son became *Captain* Henry Whitener, commander of a company in the Lincoln County, North Carolina, militia. He and his volunteers fought in the critical battles of King's Mountain and Cowpens, where they helped break British military power in the South.

Less well known, Capt. Whitener made an alliance with his friendly neighbors, the Catawbas, against the British-aligned Cherokees. He took part in the 1782 Cherokee Expedition and burned many villages (this was against another part of my ancestral family). Incredibly, my ancestor, Captain Whitener, may have been the guardian of the last survivors of Cahokia.

No fiction from the minds of men can ever surpass the profound twists and turns of history and the foolishness of the Mind of God.

Mark Nickless
co-author *Chasing Dragons*

Mark Nickless & Laurie Bonner-Nickless

ADDITIONAL SUPPORTIVE PROOFS

There are many additional supporting proofs of pre-Columbian Ming Chinese contact with North America, including more about the Chinese origin of the Piasa.

But, as Luo might have put it—"those details must be left for other chapters" …chapters which can be found in Laurie's full translation of the final fifteen chapters of Luo's epic—*To the Gates of Fengtu.*

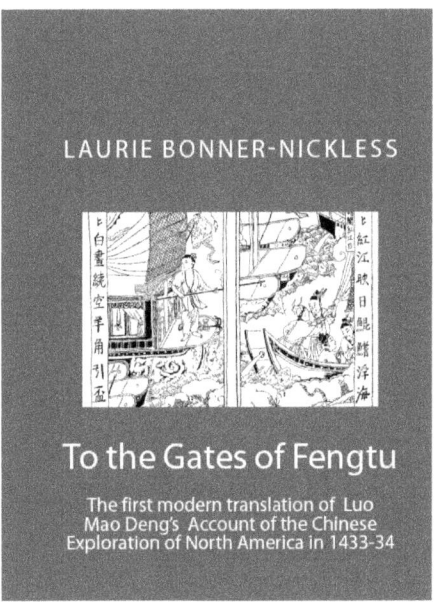

"*TO THE GATES OF FENG TU* is the definitive proof that China discovered America"
Gavin Menzies, author of *1421- THE YEAR CHINA DISCOVERED AMERICA.*
(Available through Amazon.com)
and

《郑和发现美洲之 新解》
(A new explanation of Zheng He's discovery of America)
(Available only in Mandarin.)

RELATED READING

Andro, Anatole. *THE 1421 HERESY An Investigation Into The Ming Chinese Maritime Survey of the World.* Bloomington, Indiana: Authorhouse, 2005.

Levathes, Louise. *WHEN CHINA RULED THE SEAS.* Oxford University Press: Oxford, 1994.

Menzies, Gavin. *1421-- THE YEAR CHINA DISCOVERED AMERICA.* Transworld Publishers, Great Britain, 2002.

Harris, Hendon M. Edited and Abridged by Rees, Charlotte Harris. *THE ASIATIC FATHERS OF AMERICA Chinese Discovery & Colonization of Ancient America.* Warwick House Publishers: Lynchburg, Virginia, 2006.

RELATED WEBSITES

S.L. Lee –www.asiawind.com

1421 The Year China Discovered America- www.1421.tv

The Examiner- www.examiner.co/native-americanhistory-in-national/richardthornton

Charlotte Rees- www.asiaticfathers.com
www.HarrisMaps.com

Diogenes Research – http://www.diogenesresearch.org/English/index.htm

IS MORE EVIDENCE OUT THERE?

We believe that there is good reason to think so. For example, we found this unexplained old photograph in the village museum in Elsah, Illinois that appears to show a dragon's foot carved into a prepared stone surface that appears to have been covered in plaster, as Luo described.

Do you possess any old photographs or artifacts that you have reason to believe are connected to the Piasa? We are particularly interested in information about any such items or photographs from the Cahokia, Elsah and Grafton areas in Illinois, from the Arcadia Valley in Eastern Missouri, and from along the Illinois and Mississippi Rivers.

Contact us at: thenicklessfamily@gmail.com

We can also be contacted through this book's web page on Amazon.com, and via links in Gavin Menzies' 1421 and 1434 web sites.

BIBLIOGRAPHY

Burns, Louis F. *OSAGE INDIAN CUSTOM AND MYTHS*, Tuscaloosa, Alabama: The University of Alabama Press, 1984.

Chien, Chao C. *THE HUNT FOR THE DRAGON, 2ND EDITION.* Diogenes Research: e-book, copyrights 2012, 2017, 2018.

Dias-Granados, Carol and Duncan, James R. *THE PETROGLYPHS AND PICTOGRAPHS OF MISSOURI.* Tuscaloosa, Alabama: The University of Alabama Press, 2000.

Farley, Gloria. *INSCRIPTIONS FROM MID-AMERICA.* Paper No. 69, Epigraphic Society Occasional Papers, Volume 3/2, 1976.

Foster, Stanley O. M.D., M.P.H. Photograph of man with severe hemorrhagic-type smallpox. (Bangladesh, 1975) By CDC/World Health Organization; - This media comes from the Centers for Disease Control and Prevention's Public Health Image Library (PHIL), with identification number #7725.

Hosmer, Charles B. Jr. and Williams, Paul O. *ELSAH; A HISTORICAL GUIDEBOOK*, Fifth Edition, Revised. Elsah, Illinois: Historic Elsah Foundation, 1986.

Howatt, Dr. Michael. Personal correspondence.

LaSalle, Nicholas de. *THE LA SALLE EXPEDITION ON THE MISSISSIPPI RIVER.* Edited by William C. Foster. Translated by Johanna L. Warren. Texas State Historical Association, Austin, 2003.

Lewis, Henry. *DAS ILLUSTRIRTE MISSISSIPPITHAL.* Dusseldorf: Arnz and Company, 1854.

Luo, Mao Deng. *AN ACCOUNT OF THE WESTERN WORLD VOYAGES OF THE SAN BAO EUNUCH.* China, 1585.

Mac Adams, William. *RECORDS OF ANCIENT RACES IN THE MISSISSIPPI VALLEY.* St. Louis, Missouri: C. R. Barnes

Publishing Company, 1887.

Maruna, Scott. *THE CURIOUS PERSON'S GUIDE TO THE HISTORY AND MYSTERY OF THE PIASA BIRD.* Jacksonville, Illinois: Swamp Gas Book Company. 2005

Masthay, Carl, editor. *KASKASKIA ILLINOIS-TO-FRENCH DICTIONARY*, St. Louis, Missouri. 2002.

Rees, Charlotte Harris. *Secret Maps of the Ancient World.* Bloomington, Indiana: Authorhouse, 2008.

rootsweb.com/~kygenweb/kybio/green/semple.j.ixi

Thornton, Richard. Personal correspondence.

Townsend, Richard F., General ed., Robert S. Sharp, ed. *HERO, HAWK, AND OPEN HAND.* New Haven and London; Yale University Press, 2004.

Transcript of interview with Mr. Ed Johnston, age 89, 10 June, 1977.

Wegmann, Larry. Personal correspondence.

White, A. J. & R. Stevens, Lora & Lorenzi, Varenka & Munoz, Samuel & Lipo, Carl & Schroeder, Sissel. (2018). An evaluation of fecal stanols as indicators of population change at Cahokia, Illinois. Journal of Archaeological Science. 93. 129-134. 10.1016/j.jas.2018.03.009. Also, this can be read at https://www.researchgate.net/publication/324869183_An_evaluation_of_fecal_stanols_as_indicators_of_population_change_at_Cahokia_Illinois

Willey, P., and D. H. Ubelaker. Photograph. *NOTCHED TEETH FROM THE TEXAS PANHANDLE. Journal of the Washington Academy of Sciences* Vol. 66, No. 4 (DECEMBER, 1976), pp. 239-246 https://www.jstor.org/stable/pdf/24536692.pdf?seq=1#page_scan_tab_contents

Mark Nickless & Laurie Bonner-Nickless

www.ingramcontent.com/pod-product-compliance
Lightning Source LLC
Chambersburg PA
CBHW052057110526
44591CB00013B/2256